The Center *of* All Things

Wake Up Your Soul through a Love Affair With God

Gila Jedwab

The Center of All Things
Copyright ©2023 Gila Jedwab All Rights Reserved.
Library of Congress Control Number: 2023917440
ISBN – Paperback: 979-8-9878220-4-3
ISBN – Electronic book: 979-8-9878220-5-0
ISBN – Audiobook: 979-8-9878220-3-6
Second Edition: September 2023

Starseed Metaphysical Shop Publishing is an imprint of Starseed Metaphysical Shop LLC
starseedmetaphysicalshop.com
lauraleone@starseedmetaphysicalshop.com

No part of this book may be reproduced or transmitted in any form or by any means, electronic or mechanical, without permission in writing.

Acknowledgments

To God. Thank you for always being available to listen. Thank you for bringing me to this point. I am grateful. You know what You are to me.

To my Husband, Josh. Thank you for being my Constant Catalyst. Thank you for building a door to my writing room. Thank you for always making me laugh. I love you with my whole heart. Who are you?

To my Kids, Sara Raizel and Ezra, Kaila and David and Avery, Eli and Mordechai. Thank you for choosing me. Thank you for surprising and enchanting me as you develop into fuller expressions of yourselves. I love you with all my life and my entire, entire existence.

To my Parents, Rabbi Samuel and Soni Sandhaus. Thank you for giving me life, love and support. Everything I am is from you. Thank you for raising us in Scranton. I loved growing up there.

To my Siblings, Shifra and Yaakov. Miryam and Alex. Moshe and Malkie. Leah and Shua. Sarah and Ben. Mordy. Dina and Alon. Jill and Shalom. Thank you for jumping down here with me this time around to be my spiritual gangster clan.

To my In-laws, Dr. Jack & Lorna Jedwab. Thank you for giving me Josh and for your constant encouragement and support.

To my Staff. Rifky, Anna, Hanna, Shana and Esti. Thank you for making my life easy and my days fun. Our office is my happy place.

To Maricella. Thank you for my sparkling home and your pure heart.

To Sophie. Thanks for all the love you gave the kids.

To Laura. The Starseed that came into my life at just the right time. ♡

To Dr. Aaron Lewis. Thank you for literally dropping down from my vibrational vortex. Texting you was the most divine impulse I have ever received.

To Travis. Thank you for being miene tiere.

To you, my Reader. Thank you for picking up this book. I hope your heart feels as much reading it as mine did writing it.

To The Lubavitcher. Thank you for your vision.

To Atma. Always in our hearts.

PREFACE TO MY SECOND EDITION

Something inside me snapped open in March of 2020. During the 2-week lockdown.

I remember the exact moment of this Sudden Awakening. I was standing in the kitchen. My son-in-law was to the left of me. He spoke the word, PANDEMIC. It was the first time I heard it said out loud.

The word left his mouth in slow-motion. It bounced and ricocheted off my soul. A single word boomeranged back.

It lit up the grid of my entire consciousness: BULL SHIT.

A dormant part of me was suddenly jolted awake. And there was no going back.

Ever since that moment, I have wrestled for a reason as to why I KNEW the pandemic was bullshit while the majority of the world did not.

The only answer that consistently comes back to me, and satisfies me, is…this book.

Why this book?

This book, the writing and rewriting of it, made me contemplate, almost daily, my deep love affair with God.

Covid was an assault on God. And because God became Hyper-Real to me through the writing of this book, I understood that assault --immediately.

Much like the Tower of Babel, this Biblical-Serpent-Primordial Enemy surfaced its ugly head in its final attempt to wrestle planetary control from the Hands of God.

How did I immediately understand this was the End Times war?

Because they came for our two most Elemental Connections to God: Our Breath and our DNA. And I took it personally for God. Because that is what you do when you are in love.

This book was written prior to my discovery of the Dark, Invisible Secret Societies who controlled the planet through shadow governments.

Because of Donald Trump and the Q Military Alliance Counterplan, these Wicked Secret Societies had to scramble during Covid and thereby reveal themselves. Trump forced them into the spotlight. Once enough of us saw them, it was Game Over. This was the strategy of the Q plan. To corner this Invisible Enemy and make them reveal themselves to the public through fumbling acts of desperation and overt control.

How was the Cabal of Evil able to maintain control for thousands of years? Because we COULDN'T SEE THEM. The struggles of life were a vague, hazy confusion because they were all we knew. We accepted that life is hard. We paid our taxes and insurance premiums, mortgages and car loans. Got our documents notarized. Acted like good citizens. What we did not know was this: All these tedious distractions that made life so hard were intentionally crafted by these Evil Overlords to keep us in survival mode.

Why did they want us to be in survival mode?

To keep us in a baseline state of FEAR and DISCONNECTION from God.

They also knew if they could hijack our consciousness through movies and vile imagery, they could siphon our vast co-creative energies to manifest their sick agenda.

How? Because our souls carry tremendous creative abilities. And they knew it!

But then something miraculous happened.

The Great Awakening.

Many woke up and saw through the veil. They refused to allow their energy to be hijacked. They chose to plug into Creator instead of into Fear.

The Tide on the Planet slowly turned.

We are smack in the middle of the Greatest Story Ever Told, as it is unfolding.

Many people, especially the celebrities, that I quoted in this book, I have now come to understand were used as puppets of the Cabal.

I debated if I should remove those quotes.

Then I realized. They helped me in my own evolution.

There is still much I do not know. Perhaps these celebrities started off good and were then captured, threatened and corrupted. Perhaps the real person was killed and cloned and then used to help implement the vast global fear campaign that came to be known as Covid.

So, I left the book alone.

My prayer.

I pray that the energy from this book travels galaxies and traverses the entire universe to raise the frequency inside your heart and on the planet.

Why?

So we can accelerate this liberation of Mankind and create a Dwelling Place for God's own Frequency here with us on Earth. So more of us can be powerful conduits of Creator Life Force Energy. To mobilize more of the Ground Crew.

The Reign of Evil has Expired, and the Time for Redemption has come Due.

Who are we?

You and I, we are ghost writers, co-scripting a breathtaking conclusion to a story that began 6,000 years ago in a garden. It is God's manuscript. But we get the final edit.

Let's GOOO ♡

Contents

Acknowledgments 3
Preface to my Second Edition I
Chapter 1 Finding the Spiritual Wisdom inside your heart 7
Chapter 2 Our Souls 17
Chapter 3 Breath 24
Chapter 4 Thoughts and Words   28
Chapter 5 Suffering 40
Chapter 6 Four ways to experience God 45
Chapter 7 Ein Od Milvado 67
Chapter 8 Emotions 80
Chapter 9 Contract Moments 96
Chapter 10 Real 101
Chapter 11 A Love Affair with God 109
Chapter 12 Anxiety 120
Chapter 13 Free Will 138
Chapter 14 Forgiveness 170
Chapter 15 Attention 181
Chapter 16 Kids 193
Chapter 17 Dreams of the Heart 207
Chapter 18 His and Hers Laughter 217
Chapter 19 Torah 224
Chapter 20 Money 261
Chapter 21 Intention 269
Chapter 22 Perspective of Soul 277
Chapter 23 God's Paradox 288
About the Author 302

Chapter One

Finding the Spiritual Wisdom inside your heart

Most writers have a conversational home. The discussion that makes their heartbeat faster. A magnetic topic that draws them in. A singular message their soul carried down here to deliver. The task of each writer is to take their soul's chosen topic and shake it around inside the memory of the rest of our souls. To stir up the inbred wisdom that our souls possess but have forgotten. For Brian Weiss it is past life healing. Louise Hay, the Power of Thoughts. Bruce Lipton, the Biology of Belief. Esther Perel, Erotic Intelligence. Terry Real, Whole People. Eckhart Tolle, Presence. Victor Frankl, Meaning. Elie Wiesel, Engagement with God. Esther Hicks, Law of Attraction. Songwriters often have a dominant songwriting theme too. Ed Sheeran, romantic love. Taylor Swift, heartbreak.

Every message is a thin slice of the same pie. Every soul comes to add their piece. This book is my slice, my soul's favorite conversation. It is all my heart ever wants to talk about: Waking up and getting close to God. Feeling God. Trusting God. Seeing God everywhere and in everyone. Piercing through the wall of our collective spiritual stupidity and remembering that our souls came down here for one thing. *To cultivate a loving and joyful relationship with God from a place where we could not see Him.*

Relationships with people are the dress rehearsal for the relationship with God. Other people give us the different outfits to try on with God. Why do we fall in love with other people? To learn how to fall in love with God. Inside our relationship with God, everyone's message comes together, and the world can start to make some sense. When you operate your life from inside the relationship with God, you are going to make right decisions. Especially when you cherish Him like a confidante or lover, and you put God's feelings first. When you make talking to Him, your favorite escape and most delicious pleasure.

So, what does it mean to wake up? I do not know a textbook definition for it. Maybe there isn't one. Concepts inside the spiritual realm are slippery. They wrestle from the grasp of neat language.

But this is the closest I have come:

To wake up means to crack open the stubborn outer shell of your protective ego and allow the soft soul inside to slip out and relax into the moment of life that's right in front of you.

It means blowing a hole through your own murky and limited perception and letting rays of awareness and insight filter in. It means blinking your spiritual eyes open, the ones you were born with, and looking around with the same wonder you had at 5-years-old. And then using all that calm goodness in relationship with other people and with God. To make Life your Easy Best Friend. To be alive and engaged, grateful and humorod, with whatever the Moment of Life is bringing you. In other words: To become an ever Engageable and Joyfully Connectable human being, keeping God right at the center.

Waking up also means:

- *To constantly remind yourself that you are a soul. And for a fleeting span of time your soul has a body at its disposal. And to operate your life from the awareness of that lucky opportunity. You were thrown the keys to a highly personalized vehicle specially designed with everything it needs for its mission.*

- *To be a person under constant character improvement, a self-aware spiritual seeker who is in touch daily with their own emerging soul, and humbly aware of and kind to other evolving souls around them. Always seeking to know better, be better and do better (Maya Angelou) towards yourself and other people.*

- *To realize that the Moment of Life that is constantly refreshing itself in front of you is your active interface with God. This moment, right now, is your precious rendezvous with God. You might as well talk to Him.*

- *To remove all FEAR from your heart and replace it with Curiosity, Wonder, and Trust.*

- *To slowly heal your soul from the damage done to it while you were asleep.*

- *MOST OF ALL: To use all of the above in relationship, alignment, friendship, and partnership with God and other people.*

Waking up is a slippery thing to hold and maintain. It requires constant review and repetition to anchor it. It can mean a different thing on a different day. Waking up always begins with one thing: Understanding that your **thoughts** are the **starting point of your life.**

We need to watch them with curiosity and detachment. Accept them with a sense of humor. Filter them, sort them and juggle them around. It means swapping out stale, old, outdated thoughts with fresh thoughts to heal, forgive and love your own heart.

I can bring awareness back to any moment with this shortcut: Whenever I become overwhelmed or scared, I close my eyes and sink into one bite-size little thought: **All is well.** This thought is one of the easiest shortcuts to peace. Thinking about it immediately calms my frazzled soul and relaxes my hunched shoulders.

Waking up also means using your awakened thoughts in Constant Conversation with God. In real time. Convert that lonely monologue you have in your head with yourself into a living, interactive dialogue with Him. **Be with me** is my romantic whisper to God all day. I immediately feel Him swoop down next to me and hold my hand. The more Real I make Him, the more Real He becomes.

I often think this weird thought to myself, "God's a person too, you know." For some reason, this strange one-liner makes me feel empathy for Him. Find something equally bizarre that works for you. Something that helps you perceive Him as Real inside the electrical impulses of your heart.

Howard Stern in an interview with the New York Times Magazine said something absolutely brilliant. He caught the attention of my soul. He said, "Traumatized people (from difficult childhoods) learn how to turn off what you're calling a soul. It's not that they don't have one. It's that the pain of emotion is so intense, they turn it off."

We have all been traumatized in some way as kids and we buried those raw wounded parts of our soul without even knowing we did that. Our job as adults is to recover those lost parts. To remember our trauma and allow the buried pain to rise to the surface and heal in the fresh air, so a little more of our soul can slip out of its confinement every day and connect itself back to God.

As the wounded parts of our soul are retrieved and participate in running the show, life feels fresh and authentic. We feel more alive. The sky is more blue. God breathes new life inside our hearts. He moves with us in real time. Our soul is the source of our authenticity and connectivity. Our soul is the most REAL thing we have. The more surface area of our soul that we expose, the more available it is for connection and interface with other souls around us.

Another big part of waking up is to train your eye to see the world and yourself through a lens of Truth and Kindness. Like choosing an Instagram filter. The practice of Waking Up is to hover peacefully over your life and peer down playfully from the Perspective of Your Soul. Your soul reminds you not to take every little thing so seriously. That this is all temporary. Life unfolds more peacefully from the inside this perspective.

Your soul is using your curious and playful eyeballs as a device to see the world. And your soul knows it is made of eternity and of love. So, there is no rush, everyone can take the time to enjoy each other. And your soul knows for absolute sure that in the end, only kindness matters (Jewel).

The texture of waking up is ours to create. It has no preset three-dimensional shape or time restrictions or measuring stick. We wake up a little more every day on our own terms.

It happens in layers and in moments and the work builds on itself. What I learned yesterday about changing my character and being more patient and more present is the foundation for learning tomorrow that I do not have to always be right. That I can listen to criticism and not get defensive. That other people can think differently than I do, and that is okay. Waking up is having sudden hot flashes of insight with ourselves — Oh crap, I have been doing this wrong my whole life. Gulp. How can I start doing it right?

Waking up uses inner chiseling tools of self-examining, self-reckoning, improvement of character and loving your body and soul just as it is. We are sculpting layers of our soul's intricate beauty, moment by moment, from a big hunk of swirling ephemeral marble. This can take a lifetime. And that is okay. You may wake up slowly, like I did. Or the changes seem to happen fast, almost overnight, like my husband. The work can only begin once you wake up to the fact that *you are a soul.* And we all came here for a very significant reason. A reason that none of us can seem to remember.

One Big Unnerving Collective Amnesia.

When I am still and pay attention to my inner self, I can wake up a little more and hear the subtle conversation God is having with my heart. I know I am getting somewhere when what used to be total chaos in my head has become peaceful acceptance in my heart. When my first instinct is *not to control the situation but to relax and enjoy it.*

I witnessed the miracle of my husband's rapid awakening. I can pinpoint the exact moment it began. After 22 years of marriage, I sat up in bed one night with my heart thumping in my chest and told him a Deep Truth I had buried inside the innermost chamber of my heart. This truth was the first thing to shake loose the heavy armor encasing his soul. Because he loved me. Because he didn't want to lose me. He changed himself and became the man I needed him to be. A more open-hearted man who could connect with himself emotionally and spiritually. A man capable of intimacy. A man who is true to his word and always tries to follow through.

I was starving without reliable intimacy in my marriage. I did not even know this concept existed, let alone have the words for it. We can get our emotional needs met in many ways with family and friends. But it is only your life partner that can satisfy that sweetest innermost spot of intimacy. To be stuck in a disconnected life with your main man is the loneliest. Once my husband woke up spiritually so many things changed.

I could rely on him to be a PERSON, a Human Being, in every interaction. To listen carefully to whatever my soul is struggling to convey, every time. To answer with love and humility instead of defensiveness. To be a steady friend trying to understand and protect me. To turn towards me instead of running away. To be reliably constant with his mood and tone of voice. I can keep him on speaker phone in front of other people with no fear of his angry tone emerging and embarrassing me, something I was never able to do. He has become *my* teacher, that is how good he is! His mood has become way steadier than mine. I never, in this lifetime, would have thought this was possible.

The gift of having an awake partner: the landscape of my heart can be known and trusted to this person I am building a life with. This miracle has saved my soul from a profound loneliness I never realized it had and was not able to name. It shut down the constant seeking of connection outside and directed it inward. To the safest of places.

Inside this book, I want to share the thoughts, experiences and ideas that have been integral to my own waking up and those I have learned from observing my man wake up. The thoughts that have traveled to me through books, people, and experiences, and sat under my nose like smelling salts to wake me. My wish is to repackage ancient thoughts and wisdom inside new language. It is my deepest wish that they will stir inside you what they stirred in me. To set your soul on fire, to set it free and give it daylight. To let your soul be the crystal clear lens through which you perceive your life. To connect to your kids, your dog, your neighbor, your client and yourself, and most importantly, to God, utilizing your own beautifully accessible soul.

Our soul is that sliver of God sunk inside each of us. It is our lifelong job to peel away our fleshy layers until we find our throbbing soul underneath. Our soul is alive inside our thoughts, inside our feelings. And then we can use that live bit of exposed wire to connect to Him and other people. When the ever-present divine spark inside you connects to the divine inside the other, that is spiritual electricity. That is excitement.

Why have we come here? Great question. We have come here to wake the hell up and when we do, to try and remind each other that we all KNOW HIM.

In 2016, I went to a hypnotist in Manhattan to experience a past life regression session. I am always trying to make sense of my reactions and emotions. I was curious to see if my connections to certain people in this life were carryovers from a past one. Karmic leftovers. But I got something much more valuable in that session and it happened in the first five minutes.

I was leaning back in the hypnotist's oversized, soft black leather recliner. The lights in the room were dimmed low and his hushed voice was being transmitted through plush leather headphones nestled comfortably on my ears. He was sitting at his desk across from me, whispering a breathy voice into a small microphone. He asked me to close my eyes and count backwards. He directed me to go back earlier and earlier. To when I was born and then to a time before I was born. Hypnosis is a strange experience. You are awake and talking, but it feels slightly removed. I was not sure if I was just making stuff up because I felt pressure to fill the silence. But I went with it. I let the words come out no matter how they sounded. Of all the past life information that came out during the session, none of it felt as intense as the emotion I experienced in those first few minutes. When he took me back to the time before I was born, he instructed me to look for a light. I actually saw and felt this light. It came in through my right temple and projected back out to the right corner of my visual field, like a circular spotlight. Effortless tears started streaming sideways from my closed eyes, towards my ears. One after the other in a steady flow. I could not form words while this was happening. He stopped talking and gently asked me why I was crying. We had literally just started. He could not help but pause his script out of sheer curiosity.

"I miss Him" was all I could croak out though my constricted larynx. These words emerged on their own from the deepest place inside me. They surprised even me. The hypnotist made a comforting sound into his mic that told me he knew this feeling. That he was among the people who understood.

I remembered for the first time in this life, at 42 years old, how much I utterly missed God. How painful it is to be here and separated from Him. I remembered what I had totally forgotten. We all walk around with something in common: a gaping hole of missing Him. All the missings of this life, my kids who go to sleep away camp, my Bubby who died 20 years ago, all pale in comparison to this primordial missing. As if all other missings are born from this one. The mother of all missing.

Chapter Two

Our Souls

What is a soul?

A soul is an amorphous blob that pinches off from the Source of all things and dives bravely down into a 6-pound, flailing, red-faced little body. Why does it do this? To choose God inside this realm where choice exists and then co-create a life with Him. I am not sure why that is the game, but that is the game. Choosing God does not exist on the other side because God is literally right smack in front of our faces over there.

Where can we find our soul?

Two parts of our body seem to be primary access points of the soul. They are easy to remember, they are the same two organs that go wild when you see your lover walking towards you — Your heartbeat and your breath— Your heart and lungs are two very reactive body parts. Their sensations make you feel your own aliveness. Your soul can be felt most strongly from their reaction.

Do you want to feel your soul right now? Take a deep breath. Inside every deep breath lies an immediate soothing sensation. As David Deida writes, "Breath is the way our bodies make love with God." This sharp intake of oxygen blows open the valves of your soul. Feel into your heart as you breathe; this will expand and dilate this delicious feeling.

Simple as that. That, my dear, is your Soul.

The vibrancy of your soul can also be felt inside your beating heart. How do we know that the soul is found inside the heart? When the Bible instructs us to love God with all our soul, God gets pretty risqué: God asks us to circumcise the foreskin of our heart. That is a pretty explicit request. Peel away that thick foreskin. Circumcise that outer layer of your heart, called Ego. Lift up the flap and uncover where the soul is kept. The heart is the keeper of the soul. Under the foreskin of the heart, the soul is waiting to be discovered.

The heart and lungs (pulse and breath) are not coincidentally our two most measurable signs of life. *Our vitals give us vitality.* They are what the EMTs are desperately trying to revive when doing CPR. The soul is attempting to cross back over to the other side taking our breath and heartbeat with it. The soul packs these two escorts neatly in its carry-on, when it jumps back to the other side. That is what every EMT on the ambulance is struggling to wrestle back to earth.

Pulse and breath are also the two open invitations to feel your soul —your vitality— during this life. We can rest assured that life continues on the other side because our soul snatches these two vitals of life with it.

What is your soul?

Your Soul is your irreplaceable essence. Your energetic fingerprint. As you think of every single person you know, you can summon the unique emotional impact their soul has on yours.

Your soul registers every other soul through this dynamic process. I once heard that our souls recognize each other through vibration, not appearance.

> *Your Soul is your irreplaceable essence*

They interact in the quantum field. Soul vibration is the specific way each person makes you feel, that no one else could ever imitate or replace. Your grandmother, your boss, your high school friend, your spouse, each of your children. Each soul stamps its own signature onto yours.

The recognizable feeling that comes up inside you is the energy of their soul mingled in with yours. It is irreplaceable. This is why things like therapy and deep conversations feel so much more intense and therapeutic in person. The energy of souls mingling in close proximity produces an electrical reaction, and no two are ever the same. The way I mix with a person is different than the way you mix. Each soul interaction is unique and brings out a new facet of your soul. Your soul is one way with your son, a different way with your mother-in-law. The interplay between two souls brings a new creation down into existence.

I once read something interesting while scrolling down Facebook. 'The soul is that same thing you see in your friend's eyes at your high school reunion, thirty years later.' Everything else about them may look different, their hair, their beer belly, but their soul will always feel the same to yours, inside that first glimmer of eye contact.

During my past life regression session, within the hypnosis, I looked down at my lap and saw a blond-haired, blue-eyed baby and immediately exclaimed, "It's

Eli!" Like it was the most obvious thing. Eli is currently my brown hair, brown eyed teenage son. None of that mattered. I somehow instantaneously recognized the energy of his soul. I have no idea how I did that. My soul must have searched its rolodex until I recognized that this was my *Eli Feeling*. I realized afterwards that this mystical recognition happens in dreams too: the person can look totally different in the dream, but you *know* it's them. It is the unmistakable feel of their soul.

I once heard Oprah say, when you feel nervous or out of your element, 'Lead with your soul." Feel your soul shining out of your eyes when you talk to people and it will not matter what you are wearing or how you look, you will feel authentically good and others will feel that radiance. If you carry your self-worth inside your soul, you can feel shimmering even in your sweatpants.

How does the soul communicate with us?

A few different ways come to mind:

Activities that produce total immersion. When *time flies* is one way the soul communicates messages. Writing, fishing, running, music, doing dentistry, riding a motorcycle. It is different for each of us. When a certain activity aggressively beckons you, it is an item on your soul's itinerary. An activity that fully engages you, enchants you, pursues you; it is the non-negotiable joy your soul came down to know. It can be a lifelong career or a side hobby. The specific thing that draws in your natural curiosity and makes your head turn, is no doubt an item on your soul's to-do list. And checking them off one by one, feels so freaking good It feels like time well spent.

The sight of a soul fully engaged is easy to spot and totally mesmerizing. It perks up your own soul. We cannot help but feel their rapture. Ed Sheeran singing Hearts Don't Break Around Here live for Rolling Stone. Jerry Seinfeld doing stand-up comedy at the Beacon Theatre. The viral video of the cop full-body dancing while directing traffic. The violinist with her eyes closed and head moving wildly. The zookeeper who knows the mating habits of every species of monkey. You know for sure that is their immersed SOUL. And it inspires us to seek out the things that make us dizzy with the same immersion.

Pay attention to things that feel like home. This is another way to hear your soul talking. Some people feel like home, some places feel like home, some activities feel like home. Roller skating will never feel like home to me. But Israel does. Game of Thrones does not feel like home to me, but The Bachelor does. Our soul is always on the prowl for things that feel like home, but then ashamed when these things make us look like weirdos. This is an important feeling to push through. Talking about God or to God out loud feels like home to me, but also makes me feel like I am being weird. I need to push that feeling aside and do it anyway.

When you turn your back on the things that feel like home, you are denying your soul the fullest expression of itself in this world. Because the feeling of home is a heaven-sourced feeling. Heaven is the most 'at home' feeling we will ever have. All similar feelings of home we experience here on earth are derived from that. If something or someone feels like home, never second guess that your soul is trying to get your attention.

Cry of the soul is another interesting soul phenomenon I have observed. I myself experienced it in the hypnotist's chair. When the tears streamed out effortlessly and were totally unexpected. My mind and heart were not sure why I was crying, but my soul knew.

Dr. Mary Neal, in her book, describes this very experience as she said goodbye to her son Willie, who would soon tragically die in a car accident. It was out of character for her to cry at goodbyes but at that time, without understanding why, she could not help her effortless tears.

When my sister broke up with her boyfriend, she spent the entire next day crying the same type of effortless tears. I watched them stream down her face all day long, without a sound. She told me that it was fear that made her break up and that she really felt he was the One. They got married 6 months later.

There is an opportunity in Judaism every 28 years to make a special blessing on the sun, at the beginning of its new solar cycle. I found myself unexpectedly crying when I said the blessing at dawn on April 8, 2009. I had no idea what came over me. I can only guess that it was my soul doing the crying. When I told my mother that I cried, she told me that she cried too. I have read since then that this blessing marks the sun's return to its exact location during the creation of the world. Maybe both our souls somehow remembered that. The next one happens on April 8, 2037.

Josh and I at sunrise

Resonance is another phenomenon of the soul. This mystical feeling also originates inside the soul. *When something resonates with you, you are feeling your soul tingling and stirring from an outside stimulus.* That inner tingle is your soul trying to remember something it came here for. Trying to remember something it already knows. Trying to get your attention.

The more you tune in to your soul the more you can let your soul guide you through this life. Your soul can become the peaceful perceiver (Eckhart Tolle), the eyes, ears, and mouth of your experience. You start to follow the clues that resonate with you. When you see the world from the Perspective of Your Soul, your roadmap becomes more vivid and beautiful. So much less painful. From the vantage point of eternity, everything has a chance to work itself out. At that elevation, you can catch God's light glinting its reflection off everything around you.

Chapter Three

Breath

Dr. Mary Neal had a near-death experience (NDE) in 1999.

She drowned while kayaking with friends down the rapids of Chile. She had no breath or pulse for at least 15 minutes. Her pupils were fixed and dilated, and her body was blue and bloated. I believe that people who survive NDE's come back carrying gifts, vital information from the other side. And God, in His infinite humor, often tasks the most intellectual, logical and skeptical among us to convey the non-conveyable to us.

Dr. Neal wrote a captivating book describing her experience. Of all the lucid descriptions she gave, there was one small detail that reached out and grabbed me. She describes walking with her spirit guides on the other side while her friends here on earth were desperately doing CPR on her lifeless body. They were screaming," Breathe, Mary!! Breathe!!" She describes hearing them from wherever she was and feeling sorry for them. She felt annoyed at having to leave the heavenly realm, and yet compelled by the cries of her friends. She decided to descend back into her body to make it breathe for them, to appease them.

The moment I read this, I stopped. Oh my God. I understood deeply and for the first time in my life, that every single breath I take— it is *my soul breathing for me.*

My soul is the one DOING the breathing. That is a wild piece of information Mary gave me.

In Hebrew, the words for soul and breath are one tiny letter apart, Neshama and Neshema. This tiny letter that transforms the word soul into breath is the same letter that represents God's name, the Yud. When you insert the letter for God into the word for soul, you yield the holiest output—Breath. Your Breath is the lit-up grid, the heady intercourse between your soul and the omnipresence of God.

God breathed from His own breath into the nostrils of Adam to give him life (does this prove breath exists on the other side?). He did not kiss him or wink at him or wiggle His nose. God breathed from His Breath into our noses and in doing so forged our primordial and everlasting connection to Him. Our original interface with God teaches us where we can find Him this exact minute. Inside our breath is where we create deep and immediate intimacy with God. Inside the soothing volley of in and out.

Breath is the first and last thing we do in this life. And It sustains everything in between. It is the constant companion of our days and our nights. Always available. Always free. Breath pairs body to soul. Body and soul must separate without it. When our breathing gets shallow, we become anxious. When our connection to breath gets threatened, we feel panicky. Breath is the easiest way to soothe. One deep breath reconnects you to God in real time. One deep breath and you are back. *If God is the Internet and air is the Wi-Fi, breath is the password.*

Breath is the sweetest sensation of life. You can inhale heaven inside the intoxicating breath of a newborn baby. I put my nose right next to their tiny mouths to inhale that warm drug. When you breathe your beloved's breath inside a kiss, you get the most tranquil feeling of relaxation and connection. Transported to another place and time, where nothing else matters. Even watching a sleeping dog's chest rise and fall is ridiculously calming.

Our bodies perform most functions of life involuntarily, without us having to think about them. Our hearts beat, our stomachs digest, our kidneys filter, our pupils dilate, all without a single thought. Our lungs belong to this same category of autonomic nervous system. Visceral things that happen all on their own. If we had to remember to breathe, we would all be dead. But there is an extra gift. We also have voluntary, conscious control over breath. We can breathe by mistake AND on purpose. Controlling our breath is powerful medicine. When I teach people how to breathe with the laughing gas nose-piece on the dental chair, I sit with them and take ten conscious slow, deep, nasal breaths with them. When we finish these 10 breaths, I am pretty sure I feel as high as they do.

The Hawaiian word 'Aloha' has dozens of meanings. I found one that relates to conscious breath (Huna.org). Aloha can translate as, "awareness of your breath in the present moment that can increase the spiritual influence (mana) used in manifesting." In other words, you can direct your creative power in the world by becoming more conscious of your breath. Breathe into the moment of creation to allow your soul to exert its most powerful and peaceful influence.

Breath is the extension cord of our soul. It reaches far and plugs us into connections with God and other people. Conscious Breath can accomplish two things at once. It can create calm *within* and manifest life *without*. Our inner soul and the outer creation of our own personal reality both get powered up by our breath. A lot of heavy lifting gets done inside that space.

Our breath derives itself from the breath of God, every single time. Wield that divine power consciously.

Breath reminds me of the mysterious omnipotence of saliva, breast milk and blood. All kinds of miraculous and healing ingredients, that have yet to be isolated and named, live inside these divine potions. Same with breath. We have no idea what magic God put inside there. Sit with any creature and synchronize your breath to theirs. You will feel waves of vitality surging back and forth. A powerful electrical intimacy. Try it. It's hot.

Chapter Four
Thoughts and Words

My second daughter Kaila was only 10-years-old when she gave me what turned out to be the best advice of my life. I got fired from a job I loved at 35-years-old and became a walking zombie for a while. One morning as we were all getting ready to leave the house, she reached up to my worried face and said in her tiny voice, "Mommy, Chashov Tov, V'yehiyeh Tov. I just learned that at school." (Translation: think good and it will be good) Until this day we still remind each other of this magical one-liner whenever one of us needs it. We connect inside the powerful truth those simple words hold.

Thoughts are weighted objects. They belong to you. You hold them inside your mind's hands. To juggle them. To wrestle with them. The second you understand that you own the script inside your head, you become free to revise it. Shake around all the old thoughts like a game of Boggle. Refresh them, rearrange new words. Kick out the old, stale, preprogrammed thoughts, especially if you hear them in someone else's voice.

This may be the singular most important step in waking up. I have heard brilliant thinkers like Brene Brown and Terry Real utilize this life-changing tool in regard to thoughts: "What is the story I am telling myself?" Holy crap. All day long we are narrating nonsense to ourselves.

> *Think good and it will be good*

Observing and translating other people's behavior, that mostly has absolutely nothing to do with us, and making it about us. We take so many things personally, instead of just calmly and curiously observing the other person and their process.

Once you wake up, the way other people act becomes *interesting* instead of painful. And if you would like someone to change a certain behavior, you can communicate calmly instead of like a crazy person. As long as, we are making up the stories inside our heads, we may as well make them feel good.

Bad stories sound like:

"I will get heart disease because my father has it."

"My hair is thin and frizzy."

"It's a struggle for me to lose any weight."

"I have to work so hard to make money."

"What is this cellulite under my butt?"

Good stories sound like:

"My husband hasn't texted all day. He's probably having a busy day."

"Omg my face looks so radiant today."

"My kids are wonderful creatures, who will do wonderful things in the world."

"It's ridiculous how easily money rolls in."

"My hair is naturally luxurious."

"My body always knows how to return itself to perfect health."

I mean, why not?

You are free to think any thought you want, all day long. It is basically the only freedom you are guaranteed. No thought police will come arrest you.

Good thoughts travel out into the universal pool of consciousness and can be picked up by other people, to help them feel better too.

Good thoughts are super-efficient, they multitask: they elevate the frequency of the world and manifest your best life all at the same time, without you ever having to leave home.

Even if a good thought does not start out as totally true, watch it become true. Surround any dream inside the cushions of your good thoughts. This will give your dream the best chance of fluttering down softly from the heavens into your lap.

Watching Esther Hicks videos taught me a lot about getting mastery over my thoughts. Her central teaching is to hold a positive thought for 17 seconds and other positive thoughts just like it will automatically join it. At 68 seconds, you have bolstered and reinforced the thought four times and given it more momentum to fall down from your vortex and into your lap.

When good thoughts turn your dreams true, this encourages new good thoughts about the magic of your old good thoughts. Good thoughts multiply like gremlins after midnight and dreams-come-true pop up everywhere.

When you constantly turn your mental dialogue towards God, an amazing shift happens: God begins to feel ULTRA-HYPER-REAL. As REAL as a best friend. God becomes your ever-available confidante. Your shimmering happy place. You run to Him like a giddy teenager with all your good news. Good thoughts are tiny magic wands held in the tiny hands of your mind. They create big things.

Thoughts dance around inside your head under your choreography, until they waltz out of your mouth as articulated language. God gave human beings alone this miraculous gift of transforming amorphous thoughts into comprehensible language. Spoken thoughts, otherwise known as words, are tiny dancers that lift and whirl you right up to your destiny.

The daily practice that never stops needing improvement is choosing carefully which words to release into the atmosphere. Words are thoughts — with strong calf muscles. Words get things done. They create or destroy. Words are the mini messengers to broadcast and amplify your thoughts into the universe. Measure each thought on the scales of discernment in your mind before moving your tongue. Always think, what do I want to create or destroy with these words?

From where do we see that words create life? God showed us in the very beginning. He did not blink or sneeze the world into existence, He spoke it.

Human beings are called the "Tzelem Elokim" (Image of God). Why is this specific name, Elokim, chosen for this earliest description of man?

Elokim is the only name God uses for Himself during the creation phase of the world. God affectionately calls us 'His Reflection' using this same name, Tzelem Elokim. This linguistic coincidence hints that we too wield the divine power held inside the name Elokim—*the creative force*. We are His Creative Reflection. God endowed us with His favorite power—creation of our own world.

How do we create? Just like He did, with words.

Creation is the very first verb used in the Bible. It was God's primordial urge, His breakout move. He placed the same insuppressible urge inside each of us. The creative force is strong inside us. We use it to make babies and art, build buildings, write books and poetry. Our creative urges do not let us rest. Then, just like Him, we enjoy the pleasure of sitting back and watching our Creations create. We love to see them take on a life of their own beyond our wildest dreams. We love to see our students, children, grandchildren or even this book pick itself up and travel the world.

Creation is born of words.

A person's words externalize the innards of their minds. If someone is spewing gossip and negativity, they are giving you a glimpse into the muck of their mind. Someone speaking beauty and encouragement is showing you their glistening mind. God himself created the world with words like, "Let there be light." Imagine the tender folds inside God's brain this phrase emerged from. Nothing fancy. Soft, simple, permissive language. "And then there was light". Nothing forceful or harsh. God uses the calm language of *allowing*. God is showing us the fine art of creation.

Magicians understand the invisible force that speech confers onto creation. Their favorite incantation, "Abra, Cadabra" translates from Aramaic as, "I create (Abra), as I speak (Cadabra)." Understanding that your speech is your strongest creative power is the beginning of experiencing a magical life. Your speech starts the wheels of creation turning. Every single word, every single time.

> *A good life is the natural outcome of a lifetime of good thoughts*

Thoughts and words create the energy field around you. There is science to back this up. Read any Bruce Lipton book. He is a cellular biologist who explains the biology of belief. You want a beautiful life? Think beautiful thoughts. You want a beautiful face? Think beautiful thoughts about your face.

A good life is the natural outcome of a lifetime of good thoughts. Your brain and body will always believe the thoughts your soul feeds it. Life will get to work making your reality congruous with your thoughts. Your cells are little soldiers waiting at attention, ready for direction from your words. They organize and get to work once they receive instruction from the command center. This is called the science of Epigenetics.

No matter what challenge you find yourself in, it will be the way you formulate your thoughts and words about it that will save you. Someone you love died? Your boyfriend dumped you? Be careful with the story you tell yourself about these already painful events. You can create thoughts that comfort or thoughts that feed fuel to that already painful fire.

I was walking late at night with a lovely South African woman during the summer of 2016. We sat near each other at a Peter Cetera concert in the Hamptons. We were the only two people in the entire audience who stood up and danced during the concert. Both of us had come alone to the concert for different reasons. We hung out after the concert and ended up meeting Peter outside. It was a magical night. Afterwards, I walked her back to her hotel. She shared with me that her husband had died young. She missed him terribly. She confided to me that she comforts herself with one specific thought, 'he is only sleeping until the second coming.'

Me and Sally with Peter

Now that is what I call a soul-soother. There are a hundred soul-soothers you can create for yourself. When you create them for yourself, they work better, because you believe them. We are not in control of that first thought that comes in. But that second thought, the thought you think *about* the first thought, that one is ALL yours.

The second thought is where our power lies, where change happens. Was that first thought true or kind and who I want to be in this world? Catch the first thought and flip it over sideways. Look at it from the opposite side. The right to question and change your own thoughts is always available to you. Just like breathing, thinking can happen in two ways, voluntarily and involuntarily.

The work of life is to notice the first haphazard thought that comes in and rearrange it into something intentional. Like turning the first shallow breath into a deeper, more soothing breath. Make peace out of chaos. Either you are the thinker of your thoughts, or your thoughts are thinking you. Think wonderful thoughts about yourself, your colleague, your spouse, your child, and watch that creature rise to meet your thoughts. It will be gradual and almost imperceptible. Change may take years. But when it finally happens, it will feel overnight. And more importantly, it will feel like you always had it.

Which brings me to my **double sink** philosophy. Here is what I mean. A kosher kitchen has two sides, one for meat and one for dairy. Having a double sink makes life a million times easier. You have one sink for each. Dirty meat dishes go on one side, dirty milk dishes on the other. I did not have a double sink for fifteen years, I had to keep swapping out horrendous plastic buckets in my single sink. When I finally got that double sink, by the next day it was as if I had it all my life. This can be applied to ANY thing you are wishing for.

Know this. The second that whatever you have been longing for comes to you, it will feel as if you always had it. This releases the urgency. Your dream will come in Divine Time (Stephanie Florman). So, continue to hold gently, any thought you wish for, and know that whenever it arrives, it will feel as if you had it the whole time. And if the thing you wish for never does come to you, you can rest inside the thought that The Force greater than us knew better. And that sometimes rejection is protection (Judith Orloff).

> *Sometimes rejection is protection*

The most fun thing to know about our thoughts is that inside them is the playground where we can instantaneously and reliably rendezvous with God. I talk to God inside my head all day long. You can close your eyes and talk to Him right now, He is the only other one in there with you. God interfaces with us and guides us all day, inside our thoughts and feelings.

God has us look in a certain direction or think a certain idea. He reaches inside the intima of our minds, where no human can access, to rudder our lives and keep us in good company. We can always turn inward and start a conversation, standing in line at CVS, at work, late at night, alone in your morning bed. Anywhere. Anytime. He is always available. I try to turn my last sleepy thought and my first groggy morning thought towards God.

Philosophers wrestle with the question, "Where can God be found?"

Maybe above us in Heaven, maybe down here in nature. I say this, God can be found, for sure and every single time, right here, inside my head.

Thoughts are the starting point of our free will. Thoughts are our freedom and our choice. No one can tell you what, where or how to think. **No one.** Free will and Free choice both begin the instant you realize that ONLY YOU craft your thoughts. Thoughts become words. Words shape our life. The way you think about something is the best freedom you have. We constantly vacillate between the energetic frequencies of love and fear, all day long. It is nothing but our thoughts that turn the dial between the two.

There was an amusement park ride at Nay Aug Park that I remember well from my childhood in Scranton, PA. It was a fleet of 6 dome-shaped metal helicopters, concentrically connected by thin metal poles that radiated out from the center. The ride went around in circles. The control panel and my young life were loosely held in the bony hands of a pimple-faced teenager. A flimsy seat belt barely held me and my siblings to the hard, hot metal seat. There was room enough to cram three of us into a single helicopter. If we sat there and did nothing, we would go round and round, flying low to the ground. But we discovered something magical. We had the ability in our hands to fly. If we lifted up the squeaky metal bar clutched inside our curled fingers, we could raise up the helicopter and catch the vast panorama of the lush Pennsylvania treetops. It was exhilarating to ride that high. It made us scream and feel alive.

I now understand, **this metal bar is my thoughts**. If I never lift the bar, I will stay low to the ground my whole life. Once I learn to lift the bar, I can leverage myself up to a higher vibration using thoughts of love. It takes strength and muscle memory to keep that bar up, but the payoff is nothing less than soaring through the bright Pennsylvania skies.

Einstein said, "I want to know God's thoughts; the rest are details."

Was Einstein hinting that the thoughts of another being are the most intimate thing to know? Maybe. Thoughts are very intimate; they are also very predictive. Once you know the thoughts of another being, you can understand its unfolding reality. Reality is the ever-growing beanstalk of our thoughts. Our collective destiny begins from the thoughts of God, but each human exerts constant influence over the direction that beanstalk takes. *Our thoughts continually merge with God's thoughts to shape reality.*

Like a video game, there are many outcomes built into the program. We are co-creating our lives with Him inside every real-time moment. The exact timeline that ends up playing out, moment by moment, is a product of this combined thought. Merging our innate creative ability together with God's is cosmically orgasmic. Mingling our creative thoughts inside the creative thoughts of God is the most combustible feeling in the world. Co- creation at its finest.

Jordan Peterson once wrote, "Our vitality requires original contribution." Meaning, the act of creative contribution is downright exhilarating to our soul. The very epicenter of our vitality gets juiced up every time we co-create something unique with God.

Our thoughts and words are tiny tools we use to continuously advance the wheel of creation. Wield them wisely, optimistically, and with a playful spirit. We are God's physical partners of Creation. We are the Ground Crew.

Creation seeks its fruition through our mortal input. Creation descends from the spiritual realm and comes knocking on our door asking for material collaboration on the physical plane. We are the physical conduits for God's creativity to flow to earth. We are the vehicles for His will to come to life.

Our task is to convert spiritual ideas into physical reality. We partner up with God all day long inside our good and receptive mood. Here is the really good news: God does the lion's share. The creative process gets easier when we understand it is God animating us and aligning all the puzzle pieces. Our physical input is just the starting point and finishing touches of the spiritual process of creation.

All the ingredients in between are lined up from Above. Stay in receptive mode to keep the creation flowing through you (as Esther Hicks teaches). See yourself as a member of the ground crew helping to land the plane, not as the solitary pilot flying the plane alone.

> *Our task is to convert spiritual ideas into physical reality*

Elizabeth Gilbert described this collaboration process beautifully:

An idea has come to you.

Ideas are sacred because they have a holy, mystical, energetic life force in them. They are conscious.

Ideas know who they wanna be with.

They come spinning around the world looking for someone to collaborate with. The only way an idea can be made manifest is through collaboration with a human being. An idea has come to you.

This is an honor.

You have a sacred visitor that came knocking on your door.

What are you going to do about it?

Chapter Five
Suffering

We all suffer. No one is left out of that party. Live long enough, you will suffer something. You will lose someone or something you thought you could not live without. This forces me to contemplate the benefit of suffering. Why is suffering inextricably tied to the experience granted each one of us? Why is it built into life? The only coherent answer my heart can assimilate peacefully is that suffering is an opportunity. A broken heart, temporarily stripped of its ego, can reach its weakened, humbled hand up to God. And in doing this brave act, it immediately diminishes its own suffering by being granted permission to touch the face of God.

Suffering is a backstage pass to the holiest place, intimacy with God. The exact moment we perceive suffering as an opportunity, it is transformed into something else: a portal to God. We can rail at Him, cry to Him, question Him, seek comfort in Him. The mere act of engaging Him, in any way you choose from inside the pain, forges a closeness that you will miss during the good times.

Suffering is a private shortcut to forge a fiery intimacy with God inside the heat of pain.

> *Suffering is a backstage pass to the holiest place, intimacy with God*

A patient of mine was telling me about her young son that was diagnosed with Juvenile

Diabetes. She said the beginning was hell, learning how to care for him and always worrying about him in school. But after a while the whole thing became routine. I will never forget what she told me next. She told me she misses the *extreme closeness* she felt with God at the terrifying and uncertain beginning. Suffering gives you front row, VIP, access to God. You did not ask for this suffering, but you sure as hell do not want to waste that ticket while it is in your hand.

> *Suffering itself can give life meaning*

Holocaust Survivor Victor Frankl A'H in his book, *Man's Search For Meaning*, taught us not to go out and look for suffering, but when suffering shows up at your door, do not squander it. *Suffering itself* can give life meaning. In the way we endure it and accept it and use it to transform ourselves. It is one of the three things, Dr. Frankl postulates, that gives our lives meaning. It is easy to understand how the *work we work* and the *love we love* can make us feel alive and bursting with meaning.

But suffering? How does suffering make me feel like I have added something meaningful to the world or helped the other? Suffering can provide a different type of meaning altogether, internal meaning. The amount of closeness to God that was earned during the suffering, measured in increments of proximity we advanced towards our Creator, is the most meaningful feeling out there.

Only after I had suffered my own unique set of suffering, did I realize that the most meaningful thing I did was to use my suffering productively; to wake up my soul, improve my character, be more grateful, more humble, and to deepen my relationship with God. Suffering puts the overinflated ego back in its place and reminds us that God is at the helm. The greatest meaning, I have ever felt is having come face to face with God inside my pain and not blowing the opportunity to feel His warm, comforting breath on my cheek.

King David repeats the same line, four times inside Psalm 107, after he describes different scenarios of extreme distress. King David says, "When they cried out from within their pain—from their suffering He would save them." Maybe THIS is the whole point. Maybe God in his infinite kindness does not want a single one of us to leave this life without the opportunity to get close to Him. The key is *remembering* to do this at a time when it is the absolute hardest: while swallowed inside pain.

The ones that do not ever reach up from inside the pain risk morphing into the worst energy out there, bitterness. When we reach up to God, we break the cycle of self- pity and narrowness of spirit that come from prolonged wallowing inside suffering. Dr. Edith Eger teaches this lesson in her book, *The Choice.* She says, instead of asking life, *Why me?* Ask instead, *What next?* This second question keeps you moving forward, fueled by hope for what is waiting around life's corner. Reaching up to God with the second question invites gratitude and mystery back into your life.

The pain releases most of its grip when we reach up to Him from inside our isolation and quiet desperation. Even if all you have strength to do is turn your eyeballs in that direction. *Do it.* Once the suffering starts to abate, we can sustain that closeness to God by replacing the suffering, thought by thought, with gratitude. Swap out the heavy thoughts of suffering, one by one, with lighter thoughts of gratitude.

The Center of All Things

Dr. Edith Eger taught me life-changing concepts about suffering in an interview with Oprah. She said, after any type of trauma takes place, look around for *what remains*. This is the singular instruction needed to go on with your life. The ground zero of filtering excitement back into your life after any loss is to look left and right for what remains and thank God out loud for it. And make this thing the foundation upon which you build life anew.

Remember, whatever deep love you have experienced in your life, whether you were on the giving end or on the receiving end, you can revive the feeling inside your heart anytime you want. It is yours to feel forever. Love is an energy that is never lost; activating your thoughts and memories can make them swirl fresh inside your heart. Hellen Keller said, "What we have once enjoyed we can never lose. All that we love deeply, becomes part of us."

Chapter Six

Four ways to experience God

1. INSIDE NATURE (to feel God's comfort)

God hides Himself inside nature. Google 'grass cell under a microscope' and see the smiley face hidden inside the cross section of every blade of grass. Or type in the words "Forest Bathing;" a practice that invites you to slowly experience the forest through all your senses as a form of healing therapy. Feeling God inside nature is a well-known Kabbalistic idea. Many Holy Rabbis went into the forest to practice Hitbodedut, self-secluded communion with God.

I wanted to remind my senses how good nature feels, so I went outside early and barefoot on a warm summer morning last week to help me write this. I closed my eyes and let myself be still as I felt the wet grass under my naked feet. The birds chirped their playful exchanges above my head. The warm wind laid a weighted blanket on my exposed skin. The rhythmic shushing from the dense trees, as their lush leaves moved to the choreography of the wind, filled my ear. The heady perfume of carefree summer hung thick in the air, piped directly down from heaven. My body's senses filtered and distilled the comforting presence of God's raw energy. It entered my pores and made my follicles tingle.

God communes comfort to every single one of our senses through nature. He mutes, filters and expresses

Himself through the natural elements all around us. We love to bring nature inside, for our furniture to be wood and our countertops to be granite. In these ways, we can feel Him in small manageable doses through our senses and not be overwhelmed. He has birds sing different melodies into our ears. Waves a wild and crazy hello with the leaves on trees. Soothes our frayed nerves to sleep with the rhythmic lullaby of crickets. Tranquilizes and coats the bronchial branches of our lungs with the salty air of the ocean. He finds endless and creative ways of slipping Himself gently into our system.

I can also feel God inside the coziness of my early morning bed. I have never read about this in any Kabbalistic books. But I feel Him inside my hazy and groggy return back from the other side of consciousness. My soul restored to my body, safe and snug in my warm blanket. He is right there, cozy with me. I nuzzle the side of my face into my pillow and sink my cocooned body into the steady arms of my early morning spoon with God.

I discovered another delicious opportunity for connection. Whenever I take my first crunchy bite of avocado toast with a runny egg on top from the restaurant down the block, my whole body tingles in delicious gratitude. I close my eyes and share the sensory overload happening in my mouth with God. We always take that first bite together.

2. SIGNS (To feel God's guidance and reassurance)

"Asei Imi Os Le'tova, Make with me a sign for good." (Psalm 86:17)

I love digging out archeological evidence of human nature inside the stories of the Bible. Relatable details that animate the people for me and wake them up inside my imagination. Their struggles and victories inform my life. I love to examine what worked for the people and what did not. The people in the Bible were real and human and appeared to have messed up pretty badly a lot of the time. Totally relatable. Their outcomes either set a precedent for me to follow or are a cautionary tale for what to avoid.

Inside the Bible, I picked up subtle cues for how to go about handling signs. I learned that signs are REAL and that we can ASK for them. The small details of Bible stories offered me some valuable tips on how to request signs and interpret them. I noticed that signs can go in both directions. People request them from God for guidance or God uses them as proof to guide the people. Here are examples of both:

1. Eliezer requested a sign from God to help find a wife for Isaac.

2. God used a sign to communicate clearly when God made only Aaron's staff blossom overnight. God proved to the world that He had chosen Aaron. Here God demonstrated His undeniable Presence through a magnification and acceleration of nature. Changing nature is the irrefutable way He can come through. Altering Nature is His most believable device.

Signs are sprinkled throughout the Bible. They come to offer comfort, reassurance, and direction from God. Nowadays signs are harder to decipher, but they are still very much alive. Their guidance offers Divine relief from the massive choice-overload we experience inside this vast universe. Signs help narrow things down for us.

Anyone can ask for a sign. The big prerequisite for sign-asking is intention. Are we asking for a sign from a place of pre-existing belief? Or are we asking for a sign to establish belief? The magicians of Pharaoh were able to perform some of the same miracles as Moses and Aaron. But because Pharaoh needed the signs to **establish** his belief in God, they never amounted to enough proof to sway him to let the people go. No amount of signs are ever enough to *establish* belief.

For Eliezer, it was the opposite: only a single sign was needed! The moment Rebecca bent down to the well and offered him and his camels a drink, he knew he had his girl. No second sign needed. Since he was already a believer, this was all the confirmation he needed.

Signs are a laid-back kind of guidance. They are subtle enough to leave free-will intact because they are easily dismissible. If we ask for a sign and then actually receive it, the human part of us always creeps in with doubt and asks, "Did that really just happen? Maybe I imagined it, maybe it was a coincidence." Our internal skeptic wants to brush it off. Choosing to believe that the sign you asked for actually *came* to you, and that you were worthy of that kind of intimacy with God, is entirely up to you. Receiving the sign, you asked for can feel scary and overwhelming.

Trust in God is an absolute prerequisite to receiving and then believing a sign. Look at the Jews who wandered the desert. They were so broken that even the most immense signs they took in with their own eyeballs, like splitting the sea, could not penetrate their collective psyche deep enough to wipe out their fear and doubt. How many times, when things got hard, did they say, "Let's go back to Egypt."?

Even the most massive of signs requires deep belief in God as a precondition, or the sign will be squandered. The generation that left Egypt saw signs that God Himself paraphrases as, "What more proof do you people need?" And they were still terrified at every turn. Their trust in God remained unmoved by the obvious signs because it had not been firmly established before the signs took place. Rule #1: if you ask for a sign, do it as a believer asking for guidance, not as a heretic asking for proof.

Rabbi Aryeh Kaplan explains this beautifully in his book, *If You Were God* (pg 13):

For God to reveal Himself to an unworthy vessel can do more harm than good... God only reveals Himself to such people whose faith is so great that the revelation makes no difference in his belief. As the Rambam (Maimonides) points out, the only major exception to this was the Exodus.

If you ask for a sign and receive it, take that as a huge compliment from God. He gauged your pre-existing belief in Him worthy enough to handle a sign. He trusted you to believe the sign He gave you because you did not hinge your whole faith on it. You already had sincere faith; you simply desired His guidance. And He felt the difference.

There are so many other lessons to hash out from the way Eliezer handled his sign:

Simplicity and specificity:

When Eliezer asked God for a sign, the simplicity of the request matched its specificity. "'God, send me a girl who will offer both me and my camels a drink."

Rivkah appeared almost immediately and fulfilled his exact sign, almost as his words were coming out of his mouth.

Immediate Belief:

Eliezer believed his sign instantly and acted without hesitation. He swiftly put jewelry on Rivkah and told her she was the one.

Telling the Story:

Eliezer did another astonishing thing. He relayed the story of his camel sign to a known idol-worshipper, Lavan. He told Lavan that this sign was proof that God chose his daughter Rivkah to be the wife of Isaac. It does not get braver than that. When I tell people my sign stories, I mostly feel like an idiot. I would never have the courage to tell anything deeply spiritual to a non-believer.

Eliezer recounted to Lavan another brave detail. He said, "I was talking to my heart" right before he encountered Rivkah. Inside this verse, we glimpse the intimate way Eliezer conversed with God. Eliezer talked to God as if He was a tiny man living inside his heart. Eliezer disclosed this vulnerable practice to a hardened non-believer. A detail that a skeptic could use to discredit his whole story. But Eliezer told it anyway, in the hopes of penetrating Lavan's heart. Lesson: That kind of humble vulnerability and bravery penetrates hearts.

I would like to be brave enough to tell you two of my sign stories:

I was 21, when I asked for my first sign. I was about to get married, and I was terrified and unsure. I have no idea how I even knew to ask for a sign. But I did. It must have come from my soul, who is a lot older and wiser than me.

My older sister, Shifra, randomly found her husband's face in a picture inside her Israel album. All my siblings spent a gap year of college abroad, in Israel, and took lots of pictures (back in the days of picture albums). She spotted her husband's face among the men dancing in a circle inside the old city of Jerusalem at a Simchat Beit Hashoeva party held on Sukkot. We all thought it was crazy that she had taken an accidental picture of her husband before they even met.

Later that night, I said to my heart, "If I am supposed to marry Josh, let me find him in my Israel album." Pretty risky request. I have no idea where it came from.

I went through my album once. Nothing. I felt disappointment drop into my chest. Something prompted me to look again. The second time a flash of skin caught my eye. I thought I saw what looked to be... Josh's hand? Now, Josh has very distinct hands. They are just like his father's: small, square, and hairless. They are unmistakable. I showed the picture to Josh. "Yes, of course that's my hand and that's the front of my hair and the red polo shirt I wore that night." And even crazier, this picture was taken at the exact same location and exact same event in the old city of Jerusalem, exactly two years later. I had inadvertently photographed Josh dancing in that same circle, just like my sister. My sign came to me sealed and delivered. I remember closing the album in a stunned state of shock. I am still in shock. It never wore off.

I keep this picture hanging on the door of my fridge in a protective plastic frame. I look at Josh's hand, hair, and red shirt all the time, and smile up at God. The thing about having a sign delivered is that it becomes a touchstone to reach back on.

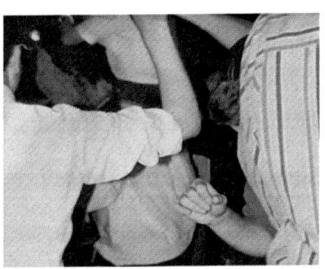

Josh's hand

Whenever Josh and I struggle and I question us being together, that picture reminds me of my Divine reassurance. My personal Exodus that I may not have been worthy of receiving at the time but try to make myself worthy of today. A sign that means more to me today, 24 years later, because I have used it well. I have used it during the hard times, to trust with absolute faith that God brought us together. Now, I know this may sound crazy, but this sign feels like my private anchor to God. I root my feet inside the grounded comfort and solid assurance this sign gives me. The sheer impossibility of it blows my mind more with time.

Another more recent sign came to me in Poland in 2017 when I was chaperoning a group of 11th graders to visit the concentration camps in Europe. My grandparents survived these camps during the Holocaust. I asked God to give me a sign from both of my grandparents during the trip so I could feel them with me. I saw my Bubby everywhere I went, because I knew her better. I saw her in the Nivea cream displayed in the glass case in Chelmno. I saw her in the way the Polish woman who saved Jews tucked the tissue up her sleeve while she spoke to our group. So many signs that my grandmother was with me. But none from my grandfather because I had no clear memory of him to draw from.

On my last day in Poland, I felt my time was running out to hear from my Zaidy. I was searching desperately. I was walking up and down Lubartowska street in Lublin looking for anything somehow related to him. I was being ridiculous.

I came back inside the Yeshiva building feeling defeated. I sat down next to Jackie, one of the girls on the trip. The day before, I had spoken to the group about my grandparents' survival story, inside the crematoria of Majdanek. During my speech, I said that my grandfather was liberated in Bergen Belsen. Jackie, who was standing to my immediate left, turned to me, mid-speech, and told me her grandfather was in Bergen Belsen too.

Sitting in the yellow Yeshiva building of Lublin together at dinnertime, Jackie suddenly jumped up from her chair, grabbed my hand, and took me into the cement staircase. With teenage enthusiasm she said, "Let's call my grandfather and ask him

Me and Jackie in Majdanek

if he knew yours!" I was cringing inside. I have asked survivors in the past if they knew my grandparents from the camps, and they kind of look at you like you are nuts. It is like assuming everyone who rides the Manhattan subway knows each other.

Jackie's phone rings and it echoes off the cold walls of the staircase, and her grandfather in Florida immediately picks up. Jackie hands me her phone and already I feel stupid. I sheepishly ask, did you know my grandfather, Mordechai Edelstein, in Bergen Belsen. He pauses. Then says in a nonchalant voice, "Yes, I remember him; he went to Sweden right after liberation." Which was true. Shocked, I ask," Are you sure?" Then in an insulted European accent he answers, "Of course, I'm sure." I ask him if he remembers anything else. He says, No. We talk some more, then hang up. Jackie and I go back to the group inside still eating dinner.

An entire 2 minutes went by before the awareness began to trickle in. Holy freaking' crap. That was my sign. Hand- delivered to me by God with no real effort on my part. I knew this was my grandfather's sign coming to me as plainly as I knew my first name. Dazed with disbelief, I stumbled back into that staircase alone, sat down on the cold, hard, uneven steps, and looked around. I felt my Zaidy sit down right next to me, to my immediate left, and keep me company as I cried.

My Zaydie's sign taught me four things about asking for signs:

1. Ask and release. Do not hunt it down. The sign will find you *on its own* when it is ready.

2. Pay attention and be present. Do not space out too much or, conversely, read into things too much. The sign will happen organically.

3. Be flexible and be open. When you ask for a nonspecific sign, let God bring it to you the way He wants, not the way your rigid mind wants it. Micromanaging God limits the miracle.

4. Be light and playful with it. The Universe loves to flirt with you. To sneak up from behind and exceed your heart's wildest expectations.

5. When you ask for a specific sign, be okay with getting it or not getting it. Let God make the call.

Writing this book even had its own sign, delivered to me by an 80-year-old woman wearing all bright yellow, Even her big over-styled hair was yellow. It was shabbat morning, in Jerusalem. I always feel closer to God when I am in His country. I had whispered up to God for a sign about my book when I woke up that morning, then totally forgot. I walked from my hotel to my favorite shul in the Sha'are Chesed neighborhood.

After prayers ended, we shuffled out and this yellow lady approached me and told me to come to her apartment later that afternoon so she could read my aura color. She had me at aura color. She gave me a flyer with her address on it and told me to count 20 steps down to a staircase and her apartment would be on the left. "You will see a big yellow door," she said.

Miraculously, I found my way to her place that afternoon without getting lost. My aura color turned out to be pale yellow. As I was processing her words, she looked me right in the face and casually said, "You need to write a book."

Her words echoed. It could have been so easy to dismiss her words, because signs come in fast and subtle. But I chose to believe my yellow lady experience. I climbed up the stairs away from her apartment shaking my head in smiling disbelief. What just happened? Only the inner lining of my intestines understands how magical that moment was.

Bottom line. Signs are ever-available to the believer and ever-dismissible to the skeptic. Which one are you?

3. Divine Redundancies (To feel intimacy with God)

I am pretty sure I made up this term.

In the Bible, when God is affectionately calling for attention, He says, Abraham, Abraham or Moses, Moses. When anything redundant calls your attention, that could be God speaking your name twice, playfully beckoning your attention.

Divine redundancy ("DR") means anything that is strangely coincidental or oddly duplicate inside your day or week that makes you feel slightly freaked out. DRs can be small or big. They spook me in the same way Shailene Woodley did when she whispered, "This isn't real," in the Divergent movie. Like there may be a small camera crew secretly following me. Like this whole world may be fake once we realize it is fake. Like God is showing you small breaks in the stage curtain.

Divine redundancies feel intimate. They feel like a private joke you just shared with God. You and God know how good it was. But, when you try to tell it over to other people, Oy, it never sounds as good. People will give you their best overcompensated smile. It is not their fault. I do it too when other people tell me their divine redundancy stories. Because the truth is, it is not the details of the story that make it spectacular, it is the intimate feeling the redundancy created inside you. This feeling belongs to you and God alone. You can hear an oddly specific word twice in a day. Like *self-actualization*. A patient said this to me while I was doing a filling on her daughter. Then later on that day, another friend posted a question to Facebook also using that same term. Hmm. Strange. It gave me the divine redundancy feeling w. When something oddly redundant grabs your attention and shifts your insides, trust it to be a nod from God.

My standard issue Divine Redundancy, when I am paying attention, can be two oddly similar procedures twice in one day at the office. The exact filling on the same surfaces (an MOL on #14). The recementing of a #7 veneer on two separate patients, back to back (it happened). An implant impression of tooth #12 in the morning and then again in the afternoon. The mother and daughter, or twin sisters, who both show up for their 2pm appointments, totally unplanned. Two patients, both named Shimmy or Martin sitting in neighbouring treatment rooms.

I like to ask my kids, where did you see Hashem the most today? Their answers always involve coincidence, timing, or redundancy. God's three love languages. My kids have brought me some great stories over the years.

My daughter Kaila once experienced a wild redundancy. She was watching 'The Chew' on the TV hanging on the wall at her nail salon. Chef Carla Hall was teaching the audience to make Navajo Fry Bread, an obscure Native American comfort food. That night Kaila was watching an episode of Mad Men, and a restaurant billboard on a dusty road flashed by. She had to rewind the scene a few times to make sure she saw what she saw. The name of the restaurant on the billboard was Navajo Fry Bread. She had never heard of Navajo fry bread before that day. Neither had I. We both freaked out.

My son Eli and I went food shopping together one night. He went to the fridge section to find his favorite yogurt, YoCrunch with M&M's on top. He found a single one mixed in with a different brand. He came over to enlist my help. We both searched the shelves; there were no other ones anywhere. We gave up. Then I remembered I wanted my Wholesome brand Mocha yogurt. I looked around and found one sitting by itself on a random shelf, mixed in with a different company's yogurt. I called Eli back to scour the yogurt section with me again. We could not find more of either one. We just looked at each other and laughed. We both understood how ridiculously and divinely redundant this was. I mean, bizarre. Sharing a divine redundancy with someone is the sweetest experience. To share a space of divine playfulness feels as intimate as sharing a good laugh.

I often hold back in telling people my Divine Redundancies. They feel private and cheapened in the retelling. But I learn from Eliezer in the Bible. He repeated his sign story to Lavan. This showed me how important it is to relay these Divine experiences. You never know whose heart will perk up.

One afternoon in the office, I had two patients named Dianna scheduled back to back. One, a 28 year-old Jewish girl and the other an older Irish Catholic woman. They are probably the only two Diannas I know, in the world. As I am waiting for the second Dianna to get numb, I muster up the courage to sheepishly say, "You are my second Dianna in a row. I love when God does that." I felt a mixture of awkward and brave in the silence that followed. The second Dianna got a small kick out of it; she gave me a sincere, half-numb smile. Then, my usually quiet dental assistant Anna takes off her mask and says, "I just unpacked an order of supplies and at the bottom of the invoice was a huge signature with just the name, Dianna."

I felt instantly rewarded for taking the risk of speaking my Divine Redundancy out loud. The universe met me right there and tripled it.

I went to a Continuing Education class in Connecticut two years ago. I stayed at the Best Western of Brandywine Valley. The next week, Brandywine Valley was an answer on Jeopardy. I have one story that flattens me every time I think about it. My absolute wildest Divine Redundancy. I took a walk by myself on a warm Shabbos afternoon in 2018, after a rough argument with my husband. I was feeling sad and alone and hollow inside. I wanted to calm my frayed nerves. A few blocks into my walk, I saw a man walking toward me. He stopped me, but I was not in the mood. I immediately knew he had special needs from the slow and deliberate way he spoke. He asked me, "Do you know where a McDonald's is?" I told him I did not, because I eat Kosher. He continued talking relentlessly to me, but all I heard were his bottom, crowded, tartar-crusted teeth.

The Center of All Things

I was hoping for a small break in his talking so I could politely say goodbye so we could both keep moving in opposite directions. But no such luck. He was going strong. As he was finally winding down, I began to feel words forming on my tongue. Oh no, Why was I doing this! The last thing I wanted was to keep this conversation going. But the words were involuntarily pulled from my throat by a force I could not stop, as if I was vomiting them: "What's your name?"

This launched us into another interminable conversation. "My name is Hank Greenberg!" He was beaming. "Just like the baseball player who would not play ball on Yom Kippur. Hank's wife was the daughter of Gimbel's department store owner in New York City. They were very wealthy people..." He went on for at least five more minutes about Hank Greenberg and his wife. He was winding down and I grabbed the lapse. Through smiling teeth, I said, "Good luck finding McDonald's, Hank. Nice meeting you." I turned from him and walked double time down Peninsula Avenue without looking back.

I got back home an hour later. My head was clear but things were still tense in the house. So I nestled on my grey leather couch and figured I would read until the end of Shabbos. On the cushion beside me was a stack of books. I picked up an unfamiliar blue softcover book with worn pages. It smelled like an attic. My daughter had recently ordered it from Amazon. *American Short Story Masterpieces*.

Perfect, I would read one or two of these and then Shabbos will be over. I Skimmed the table of

Contents. The word *Jews* caught my eye. Philip Roth, *The Conversion Of The Jews.*

The day was getting dark outside, and I was immersed in the story Philip Roth was telling me. The paragraph at the very bottom of page 444 began,

"It is now free discussion time," Rabbi Binder said. "Feel free to talk about any Jewish matter at all — religion, family, politics, sports —

"There was silence. It was a gusty, cloudy November afternoon and it did not seem as though there ever was or could be a thing called baseball. So nobody this week said a word about that hero from the past, Hank Greenberg—which limited free-discussion considerably."

I jumped as if a ghost had just spooked me. Did this book just say Hank Greenberg? A name I had never heard until a crazy man stopped me asking for directions to McDonald's a few hours ago? I gently laid the book down on my lap, turned my head sideways and looked quizzically at the wall. I scanned the room, eyes wide, while a resounding "no way" echoed through my entire consciousness. "Who is even going to believe me?" I thought. Well, my husband did, immediately, which went a long way towards us being friends again. Two weeks later, my sister Sarah had the best reaction of all. "Omygod Gila, you know you met Eliyahu Hanavi" (Elijah the Prophet).

The intimate thing about Divine Redundancies is this: there were a million-minute details that had to snap into place, like a million-piece puzzle, to bring it to you.

From Hank's mom naming him Hank Greenberg over 50 years ago, all the way down to the exact time I walked out my front door that day. All that Divine coordination happened just to make me feel seen, heard, and loved by God. I think back on that Hank Greenberg moment, and it always sends waves of warmth down the left side of my body and an inner knowing that God is playful as hell.

I have been writing this chapter on Divine redundancies for a few days now. Last night, my husband and I were laughing together before bed. He told me that he just found out that our air conditioner repair guy is named Renato and he had been accidentally calling him Rinaldo for years. My husband finally saw it spelled out on an invoice. Oops, awkward. Later that same morning, the first patient listed on his work schedule was also named Renato. Bizarre. My husband telling me his DR story while I was writing this DR chapter is a divine redundancy triple-wrapped inside itself. When you pay attention, they are everywhere.

4. TIMING and SYNCHRONICITY (To develop trust and surrender in God)

"The thing I keep on finding is, everything seems to be about timing." Passenger wrote that line in a song. This lyric fully captured me the first time I heard it. This lyric prompted a simple mathematical equation for me:

$$\text{Timing} = \text{Everything}$$
$$\text{God} = \text{Everything}$$
$$\text{God} = \text{Timing}.$$

All that you are meant to have and all that you are meant to experience will come to you at exactly the right time. Down to the millisecond. Every time you sink this thought, deep in the marrow of your bones, you will have Trust. You will Surrender to the experience of life unfolding all around you. This will free up your spirit to pleasurably take in and absorb each moment. You will have less worry, less fear, and less anxiety. Imagine that. You will be amused, as things playfully roll into your experience.

What you are meant to have and who you are meant to meet are already on their way to you and will arrive at exactly the right time. That is the surrender part. You cannot slow it down or hurry it up. It will get here when it gets here. On Divine time. What is not meant for you, will not come to you. That is the hard part, that is the Trust part. God knows what is best for your soul to experience and what to protect your soul from. It can feel crushing when we miss the things, we thought we should have had. This crushing feeling offers you the exquisite opportunity to trust that however your life looks right now is exactly how it is supposed to look.

When things are not working, the Universe is trying to save your ass. I saw that on FB. We are not responsible for timing. We could not be even if we tried. No human could orchestrate events to coincide. Go ahead and try to have two people bump into each other on the street. One red light and your entire plan is shot. My love, Albert Einstein, said, "Time is an illusion." This is hard for us to grasp, as we are such time-oriented beings. But there is a place where all that exists is now, and we can just enjoy the fullness of being.

Einstein also said time exists here so everything does not happen all at once. I like that, it makes sense to me. Time slows everything down to a perfect pace for life to unfold along a timeline. But I think time is even more than that. Time is a device of God. God uses the element of time to illuminate events. Events that we could never possibly have arranged on our own. He shows us how easy they are for Him to arrange. God speaks to us through timing to tell us to relax.

God is the Master Party Planner of your life. Enjoy the party. Have you ever met a party planner? Not one party planner likes to be second-guessed or micromanaged. Trusting timing means trusting God. Be patient to life and trust the clues that timing is handing you. God moves our lives in very specific directions using Timing: Exactly when we meet who we meet, How you heard the phone ring on the way out the door, The person you bumped into at the party you were not even supposed to go to.

The exciting thing is that there are still people out there you have not met yet, who will be miracles in your life! Just as there are people in your life right now that I am sure you could say came to you as miracles. Which brings me to the story of Anna.

I was fired from my favorite job in early January of 2010. I was in despair. I had no idea what to do next with my life. I was peeking down into the abyss. I asked my boss to stay an extra week to finish up some cases. During that extra week, his regular dental assistant took off. She never took off. A dental assistant from a temp agency came in to cover for her. Her name was Anna. Something about Anna's efficiency, vibrancy, good mood, and curly hair compelled me to ask for her number.

Cold asking for someone's number was something I had never done before, but my gut said: get this girl's number. Thankfully, I listened. I kept that number and called her a whole year later as I was building my office. Anna remembered me right away and said she felt the same connection.

Anna has been with me as my right hand ever since. My life does not work without Anna. She does the job of ten people in my office. The exquisite timing of meeting Anna in that extra week of leaving my old job humbles me to this very minute. The synchronicity in meeting Anna helps my heart understand how to surrender and trust. It whispers to me, it will all be okay, everything you need will jump into your hands at just the right time. The important thing is to follow the impulses of your gut as they come to you.

Carl Jung gave us a gorgeous word, **synchronicity**. The word tinkles off the tongue like wind chimes. He defined it as the coincidental occurrence of events that seem to have no causal relationship. In other words, when the universe lifts up its party dress to show us the underlying meshwork holding it all together. In a blink, we get a glimpse of the patterned interconnectedness of all things. Then it is gone.

The experience of synchronicity gives our soul a brief respite, a moment of perfect elevation. We are lifted up to a high enough vantage point where the pieces of the world fall into place. When random events align so perfectly that you know for sure that *nothing* is random. That everything is exquisitely coordinated by the party planner on High.

The Center of All Things

It was January 2017, and I was in Israel for my sister Dina's wedding. It was the Shabbos right after the wedding and it was late in the afternoon. I wanted to go pray Mincha at the Kotel since I was heading back to America the next day. I asked every single person if they would go with me. They were all exhausted and said no. So, I had no choice but to go by myself.

My spirit was feeling wide open as my feet treaded the smooth Jerusalem stone down the steep incline towards the Jaffa Gate. I looked up playfully to Hashem and said, "Show me something." A very vague and open request, hanging out there like a matzah ball. Then I let it go and kept walking. A few feet away from Jaffa gate, a familiar face flashed inside my right field of vision. I know this guy. How do I know this guy? Omigod, it's Avraham. My synapses started sparking.

Avraham is a gentle and kind soul who runs an organization that helps poor families with new babies get the supplies they need. He comes to my office in Cedarhurst once or twice a year and I donate some money and he gives me a thousand blessings in return.

Many charity collectors come to my office, but Avraham stands out. He is not pushy, he is sweet and sincere, and I like him. I always donate to him with pleasure. I had met with Avraham in my office a few weeks before my trip to Israel. We parted ways in front of the parking meters across from my office. As we both opened the doors to our cars, I waved to him and said whimsically,

"Next time I see you, we will be in Jerusalem!" I drove away with that cringey feeling of why did I just say that weird thing?

Back to this moment, weeks later, we found ourselves speechless in front of the Jaffa gate. Both remembering that weird thing I had said to him in America. We both halted and shared a moment of holy disbelief. He recovered first and told me that his friend Yaakov, standing right next to him, had convinced him to go to the Kotel for Mincha and that he never usually goes on Shabbos.

> *Carl Jung said synchronicity is "an ever-present reality for those who have the eyes to see it."*

Our footsteps intersected with breathtaking synchronicity and brought fulfillment to my words from weeks before and to my private thoughts from moments before.

I am still speechless when I think about this story. I realized so many things. That God is with me inside my playful thoughts, that maybe He even *gives* me those thoughts. That God synchronized my thoughts, words, and steps to actually *show me something*. When I go back in time to revisit that memory, it still blows me away. The intimacy was almost too much. Why? Because this was a trifecta of synchronicity. It contained all three love languages: Divine timing, sign request, and divine redundancy were all rolled up in one event. But it was *even better* because it was shared. I saw in Avraham's eyes the same thing I felt in my heart. Total awe.

Carl Jung said synchronicity is "an ever-present reality for those who have the eyes to see it." It is inside the eyes of the heart and soul, not the rational mind, that seemingly random moments turn into a beautiful love note from God.

Moments of Synchronicity are the biggest gift. Make a notebook of them. Squeeze them tight to your heart whenever you receive them. They are a sign that your soul was awake.

Chapter Seven

Ein Od Milvado

A God fearing person who slept alone in the wilderness was asked, "Aren't you afraid of wild animals? How can you sleep out here?"

He replied, "I would be embarrassed if the Almighty were to see that I was afraid of anything besides Him. —Chovos Halevovos

EIN OD MILVADO. (Deuteronomy 4:35)

Translated loosely—there Ain't Nothing Besides Him. These three Hebrew words are strung together simply and poetically. They are all my soul ever needs to realign itself with God immediately. I try to remember to hold them under my breath all day. Everything brought to you, all day long, is from God. Every animal, mineral, and vegetable. This exact sentiment concludes the famous Mother Teresa poem, *Do It Anyway*. She says, "In the final analysis, it is between you and God. It was never between you and them anyway."

In all that you do, alone or with other people, in the end, It Is Only With Him. Because there is Nothing Besides Him. Everything in your life has been tailor-made for your soul to Know God inside this place. "For your soul to unfold," as I have heard Michael Beckwith say.

> *Everything brought to you, all day long is from God*

The Biblical source of these three magnificent words is Deuteronomy 4:35.

The Hebrew text goes:
> *To you it was shown, That you might know…*
>
> *That God (name of mercy), HE is the God (name of judgement). There is None Other Besides Him.*

The wording of that second sentence strikes me. What does it mean, *That God, He is the God?* I interpret the deliberate and redundant usage of God's two different names in this verse as comfort. When we analyze the wording, we see that it has always been the Merciful God sitting in the Judge's seat. The merciful God has always been the Judge. There is no reality besides that.

The more we live inside this reality, that our merciful God is our only Judge, the only One we ever need to impress or worry about disappointing, the more we get to witness His singular influence on our life. The first sentence is contingent on believing the truth of the second sentence. When we know for sure that Everything Is from Him we become a more worthy vessel. More worthy of seeing how the Merciful One is the Judge.

You stepped in dog poop in your own living room this morning. From Him.
You won the peer review case against the crazy old lady. From Him.

> *When we know for sure that Everything Is from Him we become a more worthy vessel*

Your hair frizzes up in the slightest humidity. From Him.

Your business is successful. From Him.

You have an 80-year-old neighbor who blasts classical music. From Him.

They finally moved away. From Him. Your

kids are cute. From Him.

Your $6000 dental air compressor unit died yesterday. From Him.

When you believe that ALL is from Him, you start to trust that even in dog poop, there is kindness. You train your mind to see that this annoying or terrible thing that happened could always be worse and the reasons materialize inside your head as to how there was actually kindness in this thing that happened. Living with an EOM mindset is similar to the practice of Radical Acceptance. Radical Acceptance is a Buddhist idea. It says, I completely accept, from the depths of my soul, whatever is happening. I stop resisting reality. I suffer less because I have placed my foot, not just in dog poop, but in the most important step of healing, acceptance. Acceptance that lets you rest your weary, overworked head in the lap of God.

In my mind, acceptance sounds like this: "He's got this, He has a reason, I don't know His reason, I may never know His reason, But I trust Him. All is well. I am ok." I suddenly realize that I could have tracked poop all through the house, but I did not, and I am grateful. What next? Go clean my shoe.

When you practice Radical Acceptance, you place an uncomfortable reality into God's hands and say, "Your plan, not mine." My soul can rest knowing that all the events that have ever happened and will ever happen are all Him. And He loves me more than my husband and mother and dog combined. He gazes at me adoringly while I drool in my sleep. He holds a small picture of me in the palm of His hand and glances down at it and smiles. That kind of love. So I accept the circumstances even as I do not understand them. My calm mind immediately starts looking for ways to be grateful.

There is a phrase from the Gemara that says **Hakol bi'day shamayim chutz m'yirat shamayim**.

Everything is in the Hands of Heaven except for Awe of Heaven. The absolute and only thing that is ever in our hands is choosing awe over anger, acceptance over bitterness. Our Awe in response to all things is what belongs to us; we control nothing else. Not one single other thing. We do things all day long. We do and we try and we hope and we pray but not one outcome is in our control. Our response to the unfolding events of life is all we ever own.

As long as we live on the flip side of Heaven, we will have questions. That is the strange deal we signed in our collective amnesia contract

The Klausenberger Rav (R' Yekutiel Yehuda Halberstam) lost his wife, their 11 children, his parents and siblings and all his grandchildren in the Holocaust. 150 people. He vowed in the concentration camps that if he would survive, he would dedicate the rest of his life to saving lives. He did survive. The sole survivor of his entire

Family. And he kept his word. He emigrated to Israel and opened the Laniado Hospital in Netanya. A person once asked him, "Do you have any questions of God?" He said, "Yes, I do, and I am sure God would sit down with me and answer all of them. But I prefer to be down here with the questions than up there with the answers." The Klausenberger Rebbe saw the innate value Life itself gives us from living inside the questions: the chance to choose trust and acceptance even after the worst has happened. He saw the golden opportunity available to us exclusively down here, on this confusing earth: the opportunity to acquire for ourselves Radical Acceptance within our soul and carry that spiritual gain back with us to the other side.

The Klausenberger Rav made a beautiful combination. He merged "What next?" thinking with the art of holding unanswered questions suspended within his soul. He went on to accomplish impossible dreams. That is a solid formula to lean on when any of us suffer. Keep moving, keep trusting, keep dreaming. There is Nothing But Him and one day, He will sit down with us and answer all our questions.

I had my own type of Nothing But Him experience the night of Hurricane Sandy.

Looking helplessly out my square kitchen window at the steady downpour, the streets started filling up like a river carrying its own current. Water began to trickle into the basement of my split-level home. Hours later, the water overtook our strategically placed sandbags, and our garage door blew off its hinges with one sonic boom. A tidal wave came crashing in. I watched my basement fridge float sideways with detached shock and horrified amusement. I think I laughed out loud. I never knew a fridge could float like that. As the water crept up my basement stairs, step by step, to my main floor, my panic level rose with it. I started frantically calling Hatzalah Ambulance Company. It took an hour for someone to pick up. They abruptly chastised me that we should have listened to the warnings and hung up. I hit rock bottom. No rescue boats were coming. We were on our own.

That was my lowest moment of the night. I remember trembling and wondering with a cold, detached curiosity, one very specific thought: How many of us would still be alive in the morning?

My husband and I and our next-door neighbors decided at midnight that it was safer to walk through the chest-high waters than to stay in the house and possibly get trapped. Thank God we did not consider the possibility of eels or live electrical wires in the water. I remember the freezing cold descent into the dark, murky water down our front steps. I remember my 3-year-old son, Mordechai, making me turn back around and kiss the mezuzah because I forgot to. We walked with our neighbors, four blocks north, with some kids carried on our backs and some kids floating inside empty garbage cans, to dry land and into my father-in-law's waiting Dodge Durango. We piled all the kids from our block into the truck. There was no room for me, so I agreed to meet them at my friend Zehavit's house two blocks away. My husband turned around and went back into the freezing water to see if anyone else needed help. I walked alone for those two blocks, dripping wet. The clothing on my body and my family, as far as I knew, was all we had left.

As I walked, an immense volume of Gratitude filled the entirety of my soul. It was as vast and endless as the stars I looked up at. It had no beginning or end. The sky felt so close that I could raise my arm up and touch it. I was experiencing an EOM moment. I looked to my right and to my left and saw that there was Nothing but Him. Every house, every tree, every star was Him. Gratitude parted this curtain for me. I was humbled and stripped down to nothing. I had to borrow underwear from my mother-in-law that night. I was just so singularly grateful to be alive and that my family was alive, that I was rewarded with a glimpse of something else. When all of life fell away, for a brief blink of my eye, I saw clearly how all of it, every last little bit of it, is just Him. And how all of it is so beautiful. As I walked alone, all I could whisper over and over up to heaven, through my chattering teeth, was *Thank You.*

Viktor Frankl captures this exact feeling with his inimitable brilliance:

As the inner life of the prisoner tended to become more intense, he also experienced the beauty of nature and art as never before...If someone had seen our faces on the journey from Auschwitz to a Bavarian camp as we beheld the mountains of Salzburg with their summits glowing in the sunset, through the little barred windows of the prison carriage, he would never have believed that these were the faces of men who had given up all hope of life and liberty.

When physicality diminishes, the spiritual backdrop steps forward quietly and whispers, *there is Nothing but Him.*

Gila Jedwab

Gratitude

There is no noun for Gratitude in Hebrew. In Hebrew, gratitude is a verb. *Hakarat Hatov* (VERB)
— Recognizing the good.

This phrase for gratitude is not merely a translation, it is an instruction. These two words teach us *how* to cultivate gratitude. Gratitude can fill up the grid of your energy field through one simple process: recognizing the good. Over and Over. It is that easy.

Gratitude is not a passive observation. It is an active pursuit. It is a constant coaxing of the mind outward to catch all the blessings and miracles as they pass by. You can reverse any poison of the mind by slowly feeding it one grateful thought at a time. Gratitude is a universal antivenom.

Our mind is a gratitude transducer; it takes a grateful thought and converts it to a grateful emotion. This emotion can generate enough manpower to reach inside and pull you out of a pit of depression or fit of anger.

Gratitude is a lifeline only you can throw yourself.

Gratitude is Valium for your anxious mind. As Tony Robbins says, you cannot simultaneously feel two emotions. Gratitude holds enough power to override all other emotions and help you recenter yourself. Gratitude is our magic Reset Button, as Tony says. Whatever emotion you need to feel, feel it, then use gratitude to climb yourself to higher ground. The thing I am most

> *Gratitude is not a passive observation. It is an active pursuit*

grateful for is Gratitude, it saves me from myself every day.

Each Grateful thought I struggle to reach for, from inside a difficult emotion, is a wooden rung that climbs me up to a better emotion (vibration). To a place where my mind, body, and soul can see a wider perspective. To a higher vista that brings an altitude buzz. Be steady, do not jump rungs. Climb one emotion at a time. You cannot jump from depression all the way up to exhilaration. That is too drastic and skips so many steps that you may fall. But you can go from depression to rage, From rage to anger. From anger to annoyance. From annoyance to humor. From humor to appreciation. I learned this from Esther Hicks.

Some go-to grateful thoughts that help climb me out of my hole:

Thank you that my eyeballs can turn in any direction that I want them to.

Thank you that my kids are funny.

Thank you that my staff work their tails off.

Thank you that my staff are always in good moods.

Thank you that my sexy husband can fix things around the house.

Thank you that my husband has muscular shoulders.

Thank you that my computers are working today.

Thank you that my housekeeper glides the palm of her hand on my granite counters to make sure they are clean.

Thank you that my daughters got married easily and did not have to enter the Jewish Matchmaking system of hell.

Thank you.

The YOU that I direct my thanks to is always God. Any person I am grateful for is, in essence, a messenger of God. God is the maker of all people and all things. All day long we can express gratitude towards people with the deeper understanding that they are an extension of God. The ultimate landing spot of our gratitude is the lap of God.

There are only a few times in Jewish Prayer that we get our whole body into it. It is when we bend our knees and bow our head for the word 'Modim'. Modim means professing, admitting, and confessing our thankfulness to God. It is not enough to speak that word. For gratitude to fully express itself, our whole body has to get into it. When we kneel to God, we *embody* our gratitude. That simple action feels so good.

Sometimes when I get really good news and I do not know what to do with myself, I do something strange. I find somewhere private, close the door, get on my knees, close my eyes and touch my naked forehead to the ground. I unleash the full energy of my untamed gratitude and let myself feel the current surge back and forth, from my heart to my forehead. Touching my forehead to the cold floor feels very grounding. It helps the gratitude settle into my bones. In the Bible, many forefathers "fell on their face" in gratitude. I totally understand why.

Sometimes there is absolutely nothing else to do with yourself but fall down and go prostrate. It feels like the closest thing to bringing a sacrifice to God. Bending down in gratitude, like dancing around my kitchen, allows me to give physical outlet to a powerful emotion that needs escape. Bowing down in prayer recruits my body for a more cathartic expression of intense gratitude than words alone. It seals the deal and gives the electricity of the emotion a chance to run its circuit. It is almost as good as spazzing.

I made a deal with myself. Whenever I catch myself in a loop of worry about the future, planning my daughter's wedding, paying the office bills, finding a comfortable wig, living in Israel. I make a decision instead to be *grateful in advance*. I teleport the energy of gratitude into the future. I whisper to my heart, *wherever I will be and whatever I will have, I am deciding right now that it will be good, and I will be happy with it.*

I condition my mind to be grateful *ahead of time*. I trust the *future me* to pull itself to **higher grateful ground** under any circumstance. To a place where entitlement and worry melt away and I remember the basics of gratitude. If I can walk, talk and breathe, shut up about everything else and enjoy it. I can rely on myself to always make my way to solid grateful ground.

I have the honor of knowing two very specific people, close to my heart, who allow me to instantly recover my lost gratitude. My Gratitude 101 teachers. Rivky, the girl with new lungs. Before her miraculous lung transplant, my friend struggled for each breath. She was hooked up to plastic tubes that squirted short bursts of oxygen into her nostrils. Her triumph and her struggle remind me that if I can breathe, I need to zip it about the rest. Even now, when breath comes to her more easily, she remains the most grateful person I know. She did the work.

Mr. M., the man who lost most of his tongue to cancer. Every bite he takes, every word he makes, will be a struggle for the rest of his life. He is also one of the happiest people I know. He accepts his new normal with a supernatural gratitude. He tells me, in thickened speech that I need to focus all my concentration on, "I am just so grateful to be alive. When the doctors told me I will never eat or speak again, I said, "Watch me." He developed a new way of eating using a tongue depressor that he keeps inside his shirt pocket. Because of him, I need only to wiggle my tongue around inside my mouth to experience a quick hit of gratitude.

I am also grateful for my heart. I imagine holding my own 11-ounce heart inside my cupped hands. A tilted, thumping mass of flesh so intricate and complex – it houses its own electrical and valve system. A four-chambered creature so independent and intuitive that it does not need my help *at all to* keep me alive. While I am awake and while I am asleep, it does not pause for a second. The least I can do is take a few moments, hand over heart, and thank it for its humble service to my existence.

Gratitude can also freshen things up when the words "I love you" start to go stale. I say "I love you" so much, it starts to sound hollow. I switch it up sometimes by adding gratitude to the mix. "I am so grateful for your love." This is a whole other thing: it rises up from a more vulnerable and

> *Love laced with gratitude is a powerful aphrodisiac. Try it sometime.*

intentional place inside. It turns *me loving you* into *me noticing you loving me*. It says, "I see you loving me and you are doing a good job. I have registered all the loving efforts that you have foisted upon me."

Love laced with gratitude is a powerful aphrodisiac. Try it sometime.

Chapter Eight

Emotions

Joseph Campbell said, "Every Emotion Fully Felt is Bliss."

This confused me. How could anger or frustration ever be bliss?

The answer lies in the words 'fully felt'. Suppressing, denying, or halfway feeling an emotion is hell. The emotion gets stuck. If I calmly and patiently allow any emotion to be fully felt in my heart, it is an act of great lovingkindness to myself. I am giving myself permission to explore with curiosity a feeling that I normally pushed away in fear or felt guilty for having. To sit peacefully with a strong emotion and ask it why it came. What are you, emotion, trying to tell me? And let it take leave of me only when it is ready. After it has been fully felt.
You need to fully feel it, to heal it.

When my housekeeper, whom I love, would rearrange and reorganize my closet without my permission, I would fill with bizarre, unexplainable rage. All my clothing and shoes were rearranged in a different place. I would resist this rage because I thought I was supposed to feel thankful. I denied my true feelings. I was also afraid to confront her and make her feel bad. Instead, I would quietly seethe with suppressed fury.

One morning, I decided to play with this theory and sit quietly while that emotion tore through me. After it was done, I asked it why this experience made me so mad. The answer floated up silently in my consciousness. What came up was my childhood. I grew up in a family of eight kids where chaos was king, and I had only a few things that were truly my own. And I liked knowing exactly where they were. That need is still alive in me today, to know where my things are so I can easily find them. To have them be exactly where I put them. I have to accept the part of me that feels this and not judge myself for not being more easygoing, like other people. I was able to let this feeling pass all the way through me. The next day, I asked her in the kindest and firmest way I could, not to rearrange my closet anymore. I had to honor this need inside myself and take the necessary action to prevent it. After I fully felt the rage and made a plan of action to set up a boundary with my housekeeper, I used thoughts of gratitude to reset my mood (frequency) to higher ground.

Emotions are many different things:

>Emotions are your soul whispering directional clues in your ear.

>Emotions are the wavelengths that fill your energy field.

>Emotions are generated inside your thoughts.

>Emotions are the endgame we are after – we are all just chasing down a feeling.

The vacation, dream job, attentive lover all have one thing in common. The way they make us feel. We do not need to chase these things.

We just sit to need inside these beautiful emotions that our imagination can easily conjure for us. *Take time to feel into the euphoria*. The universe will understand your request and bring you more experiences that match this feeling. Remembering what heaven feels like brings you more heaven. Einstein said, match the vibration inside your imagination and you cannot help but get the reality. This is not philosophy, it is science.

Our imagination is a powerful magnet; it draws down our reality. It is really none of our business how God brings you the experiences that match the feeling you requested. Let Him surprise you. I want to feel playfulness, security, laughter, excitement and fulfillment. God knows. I trust Him to deliver.

The emotion of **Jealousy** is a powerful spokesman for our soul. Jealousy is an indicator light on your dashboard. It lights up for two reasons:

1. To tell you where your soul wants to be.

When I hear of people making Aliyah to Israel or writing books on spirituality, I get jealous because that is where I want to be and what I want to be doing. As soon as I acknowledge this reason for my jealousy and admit it playfully out loud to myself (I am so jealous!), the jealousy loses half its potency. Jealousy is not a character trait; it is a road marker. Use this emotion to understand where your soul is asking you to go.

> *Remembering what heaven feels like brings you more heaven. Einstein said, match the vibration inside your imagination and you cannot help but get the reality*

I also get crazy jealous when people tell me about their close relationship with God. I feel an instant flush of possessive jealousy. (He is mine!) Then I remember why my jealousy button lit up. Because God is always the place I want to be. I also want to become a spiritual healer. I am not sure exactly what that means yet, though. But God knows. I trust Him to guide me there.

2. To heal a wound inside.

I get triggered by comments about people being naturally beautiful or seeing women with beautifully non-frizzy hair. I get instantly jealous. I used to push this feeling away. Judging myself as bad for feeling jealous. Now I let the jealous feeling come up for as long as it wants to. I ask the jealousy, like a dog scratching at my door, "Do you need to be let out?" The frizzy hair and beauty insecurity comes up to ask me to heal my inner 12-year-old, who once asked someone she loved if she was beautiful and they answered, "No, not naturally." I still remember the exact spot I was standing in when those words were burned into my soul. My soul wants this burn to be healed as much as possible. Fully feeling the jealousy until it passes helps heal my inner child. She is jealous because she thought she needed beauty to be seen and to be loved.

Understanding that this is a trigger specific to *me* because of *my* history, was an epiphany, for real. Wait, not everyone has a beauty/hair trigger? But then I realized everyone has their own irrational triggers stemming from their specific childhood injury. So, I can understand something new. When I witness someone overreacting or becoming jealous, I know that a trigger deep inside their wiring has just been tripped. And instead of reacting to their jealousy, I can choose to be still and feel empathy for their wounded inner child and hold space for whatever healing they need at that moment.

If they're hysterical, it's historical (Terry Real).

The drama always points to the trauma (Phil Good).

Analyzing and understanding the source of my own jealous feelings brings half the healing. I can connect the dots from my childhood hurts to my adulthood jealousies. The other half of me heals when I go inside and sit with that little hurt girl and offer her comfort, by sitting with her inside the jealous feeling and understanding why. I can be the reassuring adult she always needed. She learns she can always come to me for comfort, and this helps heal her. I have seen a subtle shift in myself. The triggerings are less frequent and the jealous feelings pack half their punch. Some wounds are so deep they may never fully go away. That is okay. I accept that.

Anger is another doozy. It comes up to teach us two things:

1. As an alarm telling us that a boundary has been crossed.

2. To fuel us into necessary action.

A crossed boundary can be as simple as allowing myself to get too hungry or too tired. These neglected conditions often show up as anger (ask my husband!). More sleep and more food are an easy boundary repair. A boundary is so simply explained by author Brene Brown. She says a boundary is whatever is okay and whatever is not okay for you. For me, 8 hours a night and 5 small meals a day are my healthiest boundaries.

Anger flares in me as a red flag to alert me that something just happened that was not okay for me. I felt taken advantage of somehow or was not caring for my basic needs enough. When I take the pause that anger is asking of me, I can figure out what intruder just crossed my boundary. I can make the repair calmly without becoming volatile. I use the first inklings of anger as a friend who showed up to help me figure myself out and communicate a need calmly, instead of letting myself run wild with it.

Anger, in its second use, can be the rocket fuel that launches you into the next stage of your life or to your next destination. When I was angry at my boss for firing me, that anger propelled me into building my own office. Once I had this beautiful office and became my own boss, I realized that I could not find that anger inside of me anymore. The angry vapors burned themselves up and gratitude and peace descended into that space.

I would like to make an important point about all emotions, in general. It is important to feel your emotions, in real time, as you talk to people. I work on this every day. Not to speak from habit or rote, but to feel my emotions escorting the words as they are coming out of my mouth. This is the art of being present. The art of connection. To mingle your emotions inside your words so they carry the energy you wish them to convey. *Be slow and deliberate and unafraid to reveal your heart in every interaction.*

You will give other people permission to do the same.

The Chofetz Chaim in his book on Shmiras Halashon said that man's power of speech is a spiritual force. The intentional emotion we carefully place into our speech (otherwise known as our tone of voice) determines the quality of our spiritual influence. When we realize this, we become more careful with every word. To get the tone just right.

Your good mood is so important. It fills the energy field around you; it is big enough to fill up your entire house. My neighbor across the street, Bianca, used to tell me my house looked like it was glowing. What a compliment! What a confirmation of the spiritual work I had been doing. I try to fill my entire environment with the good energy from my good mood and good thoughts. People sometimes walk into my office and tell me they feel the good energy. I love that. I have a plant in my waiting room that will not stop growing.

The single best gift my husband gave me when he woke up spiritually was his consistent and reliable good mood. It freed me. I no longer had to tiptoe around him or brace myself or be on high alert or feel the need to protect my kids from him. I know the Josh I will get every day, because he is doing the work. I know he will keep a space open for tenderness. He is reading all the spiritual books he can get his hands on and doing the work of using his thoughts to bring his mood back to center.

What you put into your system matters.

Be careful with what you feed into your system. Good moods become more consistent and reliable if we guard the input. I do not watch the news, especially at night. I only watch comedies, Family Feud, or the food network. I mostly read books on self-improvement or spirituality. If whatever I am reading starts bringing me down, I stop. Immediately.

My dreams and moods are better when I protect my exposure. The lingering heavy mood and disturbing mental images from a violent movie stay with me for days. The gratuitous sex, death, and violence we see in everyday TV shows injures our vulnerable souls. Our souls need us to protect their innocence. How did we let the brutal and the vulgar become the normal? Our imaginations have been filled with horrible images. Reality cannot help itself but deliver to us the contents of our collective unconscious. But one awake soul is more powerful than a million sleeping ones. So do not despair.

Emotions are created two ways: outside in or inside out. Emotions can be sourced from within (our thoughts) and from without (the environment). When you train your thoughts inward, to linger on the inner tingle, you anchor yourself to an internal good mood. When you condition your good mood legs, you can walk through total chaos with a steady gait. Relying on anything or anyone outside yourself to make you happy makes you a sailboat turning in the wind. You are putting an energetic strain on your environment to keep you happy. When you generate your own constant good mood you become a motor boat that turns in any direction it wants.

I once heard Steve Harvey say about his second wife, Marjorie, "She came to me happy." What a gift she gave him. He knew that it was not his lifelong burden to make her happy. What a relief. My oldest daughter, Sara Raizel, once shared with me a life-changing thought about emotions. She taught me something simple she heard, *"Emotions are like the weather; they always change."*

My insides shifted as she said it. No bad feeling stays forever. If I am having a hard night, I can remind myself that I will feel better in the morning. Just yesterday, after working on this chapter in the morning, I went to work. Outside my operatory window, the day I witnessed, there was sunshine, clouds, warm winds, cold rain, and even ten minutes of hail that pelted down. What a moody day! What a divine redundancy. The best gift you can give your family is a reliable good mood sourced in elevated thoughts of God and gratitude. So, I guard the input and monitor my output. I have zero influence over the weather outside, but inside, the thermometer belongs to me. I want to get the temperature coming off my body just right.

Emotions open into a communion with God. God will get inside any emotion and feel it with you. You can tell Him how beautiful the sunset is or how much you adore your sleeping husband, or how sad that movie made you feel. He created the emotion you are feeling, so He can climb inside it with you. Especially when it has no name.

You never have to feel alone because He can get inside that loneliness with you and hold you until it is gone. God gets every nuanced emotion, every single emotional subtlety.

> *"Emotions are like the weather; they always change."*

At a Tony Robbins retreat I once attended, he explained to the crowd the most interesting thing about emotions. He said, everyone has an *emotional home*. For some people it is happiness, Others it is anxiety. Others it is humor. Your emotional home is the default emotion inside you that is *most dominant*. You can often tell someone's emotional home by the type of music they listen to. Does it have a happy, hopeful, or depressing vibe?

Tony said that he saw this phenomenon most acutely in a group he was coaching when 9/11 hit. He said, "Whatever each person naturally was, they became MORE of that during the crisis. Someone whose emotional home was sadness became more sad. Anxious, became more anxious. The funny ones told more jokes." During a crisis we become a magnified version of what we already are inside. Who we naturally are becomes multiplied by a factor of ten. I see this happening now, as I sit here during the height of the coronavirus. I named it **Personality Magnification.** People who owned the travel-sized Purell before this whole thing started now have the Costco-sized Purell. People who blamed their neighbor for catching a cold now blames the world for spreading the disease. The worriers worry more. The control freaks control more. The trusters trust more. Be very intentional about the emotional home you build inside yourself.

The good news: you are your own real estate agent. Once you wake up and see the four walls of your shanty dwelling, you can move yourself the hell out.

> *Your emotional home is the default emotion inside you that is most dominant*

Counterparts

It is a Kabbalistic idea that everything we see here on the physical plane has a spiritual counterpart up in heaven. Life on earth is a mirrored reflection of Life up in Heaven. All the concrete stuff you see down here exists in some ethereal form over there: Lawyers, court reporters, tour guides, laughter, music, singing, dancing. All of it.

Down here things are clunkier and clumsier, slowed down by the weight of time and matter. This world is a material rendering of spiritual realities. Our progressive innovations here on earth demonstrate in physical format things already going on over there. I also believe that one day these realities will merge.

Phones show us about the instant connectivity already going on up there. Airplanes, about the thrill, speed, and ease of travel happening on the other side. Video games demonstrate how all the possibilities are built into the system; we just need to play the game. The game can accommodate any choice we make. Many rounds, many lives, many outcomes. The point is to have fun while you play and to keep moving.

Video recorders demonstrate that no memory is ever lost. God can always replay our best moments back for us. We can rewind and fast forward whenever we want.

The delete button is a comforting illustration of how mistakes we sincerely regret can be erased from the hard drive, and never mentioned again.

Waze guides you step by step, anywhere you wish to go. All you need to know is your destination. Heaven will map it out for you. It will always find you a new route if you take a wrong turn, without making that horrible sound.

Anyone who can remember encyclopedias sitting on the shelves of their childhood home can remember life before Google. Back then, we could never fathom having an immediate answer to anything we could think of, in seconds. This is what it is like up there. All Google, all the time.

Anything physical happening *down here* has its root in the spiritual plane *up there*. Look around you down here; some form of all you see is also going on up there.

Technology is advancing exponentially to reveal to us more of what already exists on the other side. I take the speed of our development in the last hundred years as a sign that we are getting closer to merging heaven and earth.

A good friend once told me about a vivid dream she had. A dream so vibrant that she woke up in the morning with a lingering mystical feeling that her soul had just visited somewhere. In her dream, she went up and got a glimpse of Heaven. What did she see? All kinds of action going on up there. It was a busy place. Her dream gave me visceral relief and enthusiasm. It took a load off for me. It helped to alleviate my unconscious dread that Heaven would be boring. I hate boring.

I think in Heaven there is planning and consulting and meetings constantly going on. Like a busy boardroom. I think there are contracts being drawn, and we sit with angels or with God Himself, writing them out. Plans with drafts, footnotes and revisions. I think there is an active volley of collaboration and co-creation going on, before, during, and after our life on earth. Most of all, I believe the instant we are done with our work here and get back up there, we remember that Heaven was always a reflection of earth. The two realities play off each other in real time.

Gut Feelings

Our soul, that little smidge of God hidden within us, nestles part of itself into a very cozy nook— the lining of our gut. Our souls offer gentle, persistent guidance to us in a very visceral way: through the subtle push and pull sensations of our gut.

Gut feelings always keep their eye on our soul's to-do list, and like bumper cars, they bounce us back to center when we get out of bounds. Gut feelings have the inside job to keep us on track with our destiny. God can transmit two ways: from the outside, through signs, synchronicities and redundancies. God can also transmit to us from the inside through our gut feelings. They rise upward inside us looking for an opinion from our Heart and our Mind. Gut feelings are pure signals from God. They usually fly under the radar and remain vague enough to keep our free will intact.

Science has discovered that inside our gut there are "100 million neurons and every class of neurotransmitter" (Antonio Damasio, Descartes' Error). There is brain anatomy inside our stomach lining. But the gut has a special advantage. It is not jammed up by the logic of the brain or weighed down by the emotion of the heart. Gut feelings are pure, unadulterated messages from the soul.

If we use our gut feelings as a starting point, then filter them upward along the vagus nerve, through our heart and mind, we can make an integrated full-body decision.

Logic and emotion are also key players in decision-making. But the gut unifies them and informs them. Let your mind ask your body a simple yes or no question and get quiet. When you feel an answer echo against the walls of your belly, that is your gut feeling. It will inform your fearful heart and worried mind. Your heart and mind can confuse the hell out you, but when truly tuned in to a gut feeling, the clarity is unmistakable. One of the best side effects of getting still in meditation is to become more fluent with the language of your gut. How to allow the sensations of your specific gut talk to you.

I read a great instruction online about how to feel your gut feeling:

"After reflecting and comparing the feeling of fear and my previous experiences of a gut feeling, I found that fear presents as a knot in my chest and throat, while a gut feeling is a deeper, subtler sensation in the lower belly or evenly throughout my whole body" (moss journal.com).

Gut feelings are similar to signs. They are both subtle tools God uses to speak to us, and are both easily dismissible. As I learn to feel my body, my gut feelings become more discernible. Like signs, I trust them because I am paying peaceful attention as they come to me on their terms, not because I am forcing them.

An important aspect of deciphering your inner guidance is letting go of what you think you *should* feel, and giving yourself permission to feel what you are *actually* feeling. When I learn the language of my body, I learn to decipher the Morse Code my body is sending me.

I learned this lesson with Broadway shows. I always thought I was *supposed* to enjoy them. Doesn't everyone? I had gone to so many. Every single time, I sat there a twitching mess. But I pretended. I finally woke up and respected this message from my body. I do not like Broadway Shows!! I allowed myself to feel the actual feeling I was feeling. Through this realization, I learned something priceless. It is okay to turn the knob to the radio station that is playing the tune of my own gut and keep it there. Even if my music sounds different than everyone else's.

There was once a boy. A boy I loved for many years as a teenager. He would pursue me for a while, then disappear, each time ripping off a new piece of my heart. When I was engaged to be married to someone else, he showed up in my life again, for a hot minute. In our brief and confusing conversation, he said something vague to me about getting back together. Something inside my gut took control. Something inside a more specific section of my gut, which I now call my female intuition, produced these words that came out of my mouth on their own: "Don't do this to me now." He did not say another word to me.

Looking back 25 years later, I am so proud that my female intuition rose up from my gut that day and jumped out of my mouth. All on its own. My gut had its own wise voice years before my brain had ingested dozens of books about masculine and feminine energy and polarity. My gut saved my injured heart from getting sucked in again.

From reading books, I learned that the most alluring, comforting, and safe space for my female energy to thrive is when I am **fully claimed** by a man (Ana Rova, David Deida). To be Pursued, Chased, and Chosen every single day opens me into my full female radiance and bloom. My gut, being more connected to my soul, is lightyears ahead of my brain. My gut received a hit of this wisdom from my soul that day and swooped in to save me. That man was not ready to pursue, chase and claim me, but fortunately Josh was. God bless him.

Chapter Nine

Contract Moments

When I was 10 years old, I was walking alongside my mom. We were outside somewhere, and she was talking to someone; I can't remember more than that. Time slowed down and I heard the words, "She is so accomplished." She was talking about a friend from college who lives in Canada and had become a doctor.

The tone of my mother's voice grabbed me. The words sounded slow and drawn-out. Inside them I heard awe, respect, and maybe a tinge of envy. Something inside me clicked on, got lit, woke up, checked in. Whatever you want to call it. Some force turned the chin of my small face up to her to pay close attention. That was rare, because I was a spaced-out kid.

I did not even know what the word *accomplished* meant but I remember thinking, "Whatever word she just said, I want to be THAT." And my child mind connected it to being a doctor. The way she spoke that word woke something up inside my soul. I knew I wanted her to say that exact word about me one day (Which she has, and I loved). But more importantly, and with the help of Carolyn Myss, I have come to understand what that moment really was. It was a Contract Moment. Contract moments stand out starkly while they happen, in real time, and shimmer vividly as we look back on them in our memory.

In her book, *Sacred Contracts*, Carolyn Myss describes contract moments beautifully: "...when the atmosphere around you and within you becomes heightened." It is the Universe trying to get your attention.

I was 19 and sitting nervously with my college guidance counselor at the end of my sophomore gap year in Israel. I remember her name: it was Linda Derovan. For the last two years, I had been vacillating between two career choices, nursing or dentistry. Nursing seemed the easier of the two, but dentistry was pulling at me. Smack in the middle of our conversation, I blurted out, "Which one I should do?", immaturely grasping for sweet relief from the torment of indecision. I fully expected her to issue the standard adult reply, "Only you can make that decision."

"Be A Dentist." She answered me with a clarity that surprised us both. Well, that was easy.

I got up from that meeting, walked out in a daze, and never questioned the decision again. I look back on that brief interaction, even right now, knowing that it was a contract moment. I cannot explain why I know, or how I know, other than I just know. My brain tries to scan itself to find the words to explain this feeling to you. Maybe it was the way Linda said it. Oddly blunt and direct. Fully confident. I know for sure that it was God who said those words, in that room, using Linda's mouth. God used her lips. He had no

> *Carolyn Myss describes contract moments beautifully: "...when the atmosphere around you and within you becomes heightened." It is the Universe trying to get your attention*

choice. He could not speak to me directly, so it had to be Linda, the nearest available set of lips.

God handicapped Himself. He tied the hands of his own communication with us. I can only imagine how frustrating it must be for Him, this interminable game of blind-folded charades. But at least on that day, He knew I got Him.

I discovered another way to recognize a contract moment. It is when I can vividly recall **the very first second** of meeting someone like the flash of a camera, a snapshot, framed and extra bright in my memory. I had this snapshot experience with my husband (watching him from my fourth-floor dorm window struggling to alarm his car), My old boss (the way his face looked during our interview), Most of my staff at the office, Both of my daughters' boyfriends. (Ezra swiveled his hips inside a row of chairs at the AIPAC convention and David stood up from my couch and turned around to face me).

I recall these **first second interactions** hyper-vividly. As if my brain took a scan and stored it on the desktop. I can click on them and bring them up with crystal clarity any time. I only have a handful of these files. When I try to recall the first second of meeting most of the people in my life, I cannot do it. What these "first instant" experiences tell me is that these people will somehow be big players in my life.

A soul contract often has a memorable beginning and sometimes also has a discernible end. I was on a mission for a few years to collect the missing names of people murdered by the Nazis. I would sit with survivors and gently coax from their memory the names of their murdered family and neighbors that had never been recorded. We would write each name down on a page of testimony together and submit them to the Hall of Names at the Yad Vashem

> *A soul contract often has a memorable beginning and sometimes also has a discernible end*

Holocaust Museum. This was a very painful process for most, including my own mother. But a strong force within me compelled me to do it.

Then one day, I no longer wanted to do it.

I resisted stopping, out of guilt. But as hard as I pushed myself to continue this work, the will inside me went missing. Then I stumbled upon a section in one of Carolyn's books that spoke about contracts having an end. Ahh, maybe that is what was happening. Her message gave me the permission I needed to stop. We move from contract to contract. Some are lifetime long, some are seasonal. Right now, writing is my contract. I have no idea why or what will become of this. But that does not matter. I have to write.

This contract to write is extra persistent; it will not let me rest. It does not care that I am making a wedding and a bar mitzvah in a few months and that I work full time. This freaking contact wants me to get up early every morning, which is the hardest thing for me. But I write for one reason, so I can get my soul to stop nagging me. My soul always feels satisfied after I write, as if a hungry puppy inside me has been fed. I just need to haul my butt out of bed.

The Universe gives extra clues to help you know your soul's contracts. They can be the distinct way certain compliments hit your sweet spot. There are very specific compliments that make my insides glow. Someone saying that I have healing energy, or that my office has good energy. Or that I bring the happy. Or that my food is good. Or that I am a good mom. Or that I write well. These compliments ripple inside me. They make me feel that I am using the gifts planted inside my soul to serve creation.

Kinship also helps me figure out the direction my soul should take. I once read a Holocaust book that spoke briefly about a female dentist during the war. I immediately felt deeply connected to her. A woosh of kinship swooped in out of nowhere. Another indicator light —I always adored my childhood dentist growing up in Scranton, Dr. Dudie. His big hands, his smell of cigar. Whenever I would go back home and see him, my soul would still beam its headlights in his direction. (What child loves their dentist?)

These magnetic kinships also serve as northern lights for our souls to follow. Healer. Dentist. Writer. Mother. Entrepreneur. Happy. Loving. Independent. Fierce. Effusive. These are the words that light me up and give voluptuous shape to my hourglass soul. What are the words that shape yours?

Chapter Ten

Real

"God is the only REAL that matters."
— Dr. Mary Neal (TED talk)

Our Soul is the most Real thing we possess. Right now, our body feels Real to our fingertips, but inevitably, it goes in the ground.

The paradox is this: Our most Real possession has the most intangible properties. Our soul is invisible, immeasurable, and indescribable. This drives the logic people, who crave numbers, testing, and research, crazy. Paradoxically, to feel what is most Real, your imagination must take a mammoth leap into the intangible.

What does REAL mean?

Real is something you feel.

Real is a subjective, internal reference point of the soul. Real has no measurable statistics, pie chart or graph. Real is a soul-generated feeling. Our soul is the creature who discerns when something feels real and when it does not.

Dr. Eben Alexander, of all possible professions, is a neurosurgeon. He wrote a book called *Proof of Heaven*. In his book, he bravely chronicles his NDE (Near-Death-Experience). Dr. Alexander, an expert of the brain, expertly describes

> *Our Soul is the most Real thing we possess*

the mechanism by which his brain became incapacitated by a sudden onset of acute meningitis.

> *Our soul is invisible, immeasurable, and indescribable*

Dr. Alexander is an example of how God is a genius. God likes to use the smartest and most scientific among us to briefly cross over, then come back to explain the unexplainable. God uses former skeptics to come back and try to reform their old left-brain buddies. It's God's only shot at getting through to that crowd; by using one of their own. These brainiacs return having glimpsed behind the curtain and have been tasked by God to find the language to share it with us. They themselves cannot believe they have been chosen for this daunting task. Dr. Alexander gifted me entire worlds with just this one line:

"...though I didn't know where I was or even 'what' I was, I was absolutely sure of one thing. This place I'd suddenly found myself in was completely Real."

This highly intellectual man of science described his NDE as "The single most REAL experience of my life." More real than cutting into someone's brain? Wow. This may be the single most comforting thought anyone has ever given me about the other side: when we get there, it feels REAL. It is disorienting and confusing to have an experience that does not feel real. A core human need is to discern what is real and what is not, otherwise we feel lost or gaslit.

We have all experienced that sweet relief as we open our eyes in the morning and the

> *Real is a subjective, internal reference point of the soul*

realization dawns — phew, that was only a dream. Of waking from a reality that felt so real into another one that immediately assures us that it was not as real as we felt. Dreams have felt so real to me sometimes that I ask my husband to apologize for what he did. While the emotion from a dream can linger, there is never a doubt, once we wake up, that it was not actually real.

Dreams are not that different from the chaotic world we live in; both rarely make coherent sense. Maybe dreams are here to show us something important: That it is possible to wake up into a higher state of consciousness, into a place where life blessedly feels more real and makes more sense. Maybe, when we enter the next life, everything from this life will feel less Real, the way dreams do. We will wish, like I wish after a bad dream, that we had known it was a dream *during* the dream. If we could whisper to ourselves during our most difficult moments, "This isn't Real." To trust there is a higher level of Real, where things automatically make more sense.

That, in death, we drop this dense shell like a butterfly shed its cocoon and emerge into a different dimensional reality where we are lighter versions of ourselves, with wings.

To wake to the dream while inside the dream takes away at least half the fear. Maybe THIS is what Awakening means! — to remember that none of this is as REAL as it seems. Why not look around at life in a more lighthearted way? Let your soul remember that this world feels like a dream the moment we wake on the other side. Be playful with life while inside the dream. Nothing is as heavy as it seems.

When we wake up on the other side, we get to keep the beautiful emotions we worked so hard to cultivate here on earth; they will linger inside us eternally. Why do we get to keep those emotions? Because we sweated for them. We earned them the hard way. We did the daily work of conjuring love inside a dark cave.

Our Technology gives us another format to understand the hierarchy of Real. Texting hardly feels as Real as hearing my husband's voice on the phone. Talking on the phone feels weak compared to the Real Feeling of seeing his face on video chat. Then there is something downright magical about sitting next to him in person. Something so Viscerally Real in the face-to-face interaction.

Maybe the very top of this REAL pyramid happens when we cross to the other side. Maybe the moment we drop these heavy bodies, our ethereal souls can mingle inside each other. Maybe inside that realm, we can finally experience the sweetest level of REAL. A breathtaking intimacy and union with the Divine. I do not think it gets any realer than that.

A REAL GOD

If I could feel only ONE intangible thing as Real, it would be God.

I want to feel Him standing next to me.

I want to feel the sides of our hands touching.

I want to feel Him sitting on the bench alongside me, leg pressed to leg.

I want to play footsies with God, as we talk.

My early childhood education was a slow and steady drip of fear. The dread of God got infused into my blood. A thick, viscous fear that hollowed deep craters in my soul, indentations that I am still filling in. That fear did the saddest thing to me — it put a separation between me and God.

I have learned something interesting about fear. Fear erects a thick wall between beings. I once heard someone say, "Where there is fear, there can be no love." You cannot open your sixth sense to *the essence* of the other being if you fear them. Fear is the bouncer that stops all other emotions at the door.

This wall of fear does not let you experience the other creature as Real. I have experienced this phenomenon with my husband. During the years I feared his moods, I could not *feel him* as a person, his essence, or his soul.

I could not experience my husband as a Real Person with Real feelings. And I treated him terribly because of this. I insulted him and embarrassed him without a second thought. I felt I had to use harsh and mean communication to penetrate this wall between us, for him to even hear me. I felt it was the only way my words were getting through. I remember one time on the phone, my mother told me that I hurt Josh's feelings with something I did. My immediate thought was, "Josh doesn't have feelings." This is what fear did. I could not see him as a person with feelings. A person with a soul. When I look in his eyes now that the wall is down, I can let my heart feel his heart. My soul feels his soul. Now that his mood and energy are consistently good, and his anger is gone, my fear has vanished with it. He has become accessible and ever approachable for me, because I am not afraid of angering him. I do not have to tiptoe around him anymore. All I want to do is come home and tell him everything inside my heart. Because he feels Real to me now.

I want this with God. An intimate relationship with Him, gone of all traces of fear. The only fear I want is the fear of disappointing Him, of losing intimacy with Him. I do not want to fear angering Him. These are very different fears. Fear of disappointing God is derived purely from love and awe. Fear of angering God is born of religious intimidation, fear, guilt, shame, punishment, and manipulation. All the worst stuff on earth. Many religions stay stuck at that lower level.

I want the fear-wall gone. When I dissolve the fear, the best reward enters my soul. My heart starts to feel God *as Real*. He throbs inside my being. Thought to thought. Cheek to cheek. King David must have felt this too:

"To You, says my heart, seek my face! It is Your face I seek...do not hide your face from me, do not put me away in *anger*." (Psalms 27:8-9).

King David also understood the correlation between anger and separation. He knew that anger was the singular psychic barrier to experiencing the face of God or heartfelt communion with any being.

Our face is the thing that makes us most Real to each other, most accessible. Moses longed to see the face of God. Our heart valves open to each other via the face. Our soul shines out of our eyes and through our mouths. David wanted nothing less than the Face of God opposite his own. Eye to eye, nose to nose, mouth to mouth. King David mentions one emotion that prevents this experience – the perceived wrath of God.

If we think He is angry with us, we are not able to find his Face. We need to abolish fear and anger from any relationship that seeks sacred, blessed intimacy.

Jews start with BLESSED ARE **YOU** in every single blessing we make, all day long. God allows mere mortals to address Him as You. God in the first person? The Creator of all universes and galaxies gets on His knees and humbles Himself. Why? Can you imagine a more gracious invitation to intimacy? God understood that you can only say **YOU** to someone you believe is in the room with you.

I have some pretty weird shortcuts that make me feel God as Real. They go like this: God understands what my Vietnamese manicurist said to her friend about me. God understands every dirty joke, even in Chinese. God gets the newest teenage slang my daughter tries to teach me, like "extra" and "It's been a minute." My favorite real-maker: God can sing along and harmonize to every lyric of every Ed Sheeran song.

The more I speak to Him in my head, in my own vernacular, not in the Old English, the more real I can feel Him slip beside me and show up all over my day.

How does He show up?

More redundancies. More synchronicities. More good ideas. More good feels. More connectedness with other people. More trust that everything is going just as planned. More relaxed into the moment.

The more I talk to Him like He is Real, the deeper my God Groove becomes. This God Groove is where my thoughts and God's thoughts intermingle inside my consciousness. My God Groove is a rendezvous spot inside my brain. It has specific coordinates.

If I had electrodes stuck to my head, the upper area above my left ear would light up when I talk to God. With steady practice, my thoughts travel to my God Groove all on their own. My scared, lonely, or even happy thoughts find that sweet spot inside my head where God sits and waits for me to tell Him everything.

When I am struggling to fall asleep, I notice that I am reaching for a specific spot inside my brain that I cannot locate; I call it my Sleep Center. It is the release valve my mind pulls that shuts it all down and I can drift away. Insomnia and red wine make me forget where it is, and I want to cry.

Same with God. I have a place inside my brain, an exact spot that feels lit up when I talk to Him. When this spot is active, a tingling feeling tracks down my heart and shoulder to my left wrist. When I am rushing, nervous or afraid, that spot is impossible to find.

Talking to God inside my head is the most effective remedy for anxiety and loneliness. The faster I remember to do it, the better I feel all day. I have been waking up at 5 am with free floating anxiety for a few days now. I am planning a new office, making a wedding and a bar mitzvah all in the next few months. The moment I catch myself stressing and immediately talk to Him about it, I say, "Help me, Take it from me. Let it all come together effortlessly." My beating heart slows down and within minutes I can drift back to sleep. My God Groove and my Sleep Center work hand in hand.

Chapter Eleven

A Love Affair with God

"Your love's the one love that I need to know." — *Boxes,*
Goo Goo Dolls.
"I wanna be with You Everywhere." — *Fleetwood Mac.*

Rabbi Zadok of Lublin used to say, "Whenever you think about Hashem, He is thinking of you." He is?? I had no idea! I will think about him forever — starting now.

In this life, we hold the cards. The invitation to Divine Intimacy gets mailed out from our address. We are the initiators. That first text always comes from our phone.

"I am to my Beloved, and my Beloved is to me." This love affair with God gets off the ground by **us** making that first move. The good news is whatever emotional effort we expend is always fully reciprocated. Rabbi Yehuda Halevi, Spanish Jewish scholar, physician, poet and philosopher writes,

"I sought Your Nearness, with all my heart I cried out to you.

And in my going out to meet You, I found You coming towards me."

Picture that: a Graceful God, ambling His way toward you. The gift wrapped inside taking one step toward God is the chance to see how He has been walking toward us the whole time. He has been hovering, waiting for all of eternity, for that first move to come from us: a single turn in His direction. A simple lifting of our eyes to meet His warm and waiting gaze.

Rabbi Aryeh Kaplan discusses longing in his book called *Jewish Meditation.* He says, the longing and pining we feel for the great loves of our lives helps us to conjure longing and pining for God. Those huge, crushing loves of our life do us a tremendous service. They show us how to do it. They allow us to understand, inside our heart, what aching and longing feel like. They twist open the tap for the feeling to flow and then we can turn that same spigot up to God. Love with people is the emotional dress rehearsal, the warmup. After you have experienced this intense love affair with a human being you now have ready-access, for the rest of your life, to fan those same fiery feelings towards God.

In his books, Rabbi Kaplan also speaks of how experiencing God is similar to experiencing love. Both God and Love are only understood by the heart *inside* the experience. The lived experience transforms the theoretical into the deeply personal. The mysterious becomes the known. Until you fall in love, no one can explain it to you. Until you experience God for yourself, what I write here are hollow words. The same way the lyrics of a love song only enter your ear after you have fallen in love or had your heart broken. You did not know, that you did not know, what you did not know.

Unfortunately, many times these experiences deliver their precious understanding wrapped in pain. But if pain is the price to know God and to know Love, it is well worth it, because our soul has been opened.

We increase our odds of falling in love with human beings by going out, putting ourselves out there, and having lots of small talk. This can be rough on an introvert. It is a lot less exhausting with God. We increase the odds of experiencing love with Him by going IN, through the simple act of talking to Him inside our heads. Strike up a conversation with God and watch those Redundancies and Synchronicities show up all over the place. When you initiate Intimacy with the Divine, He will flirt with you all day.

We can give love and receive love with God. The affair goes both ways.

Giving: You can tap the euphoric feeling you felt from any intense love affair and hurtle that feeling towards God. God shows us the menu, the full gamut of emotions, inside our experiences with other people. God also encompasses both the feminine and the masculine, so whichever gender has given you the best template, use the corresponding pronoun. Think of Him/Her as a mother or a father, a lover. Whatever human interaction has given you the most pleasurable encounter with love and intimacy. Use that magical feeling to conjure and intensify love back towards God. It really works; I do this all the time. Holding a newborn baby makes my heart tingle with love. I can swirl this feeling around it inside my heart and expand it back towards God. He granted me the feeling, now I get to try it out on Him.

Receiving: God uses other people to make us understand a small fraction of His love for each of us. My husband loves me a ridiculous amount. He gives me the closest human experience of God's unconditional love. When we lie in bed in the early morning hours, and I bury my face in his hairy, cozy chest, I think this is how God wants to show me love right now. and I receive it all the way to my toes. When Josh grabs me, that is God reminding me how desirable I am. When my dog, Skeeter, barrels toward me at full speed when I get home from work every single day, also God.

God is the best love partner to have. He has the three top qualities of all good boyfriends:

1. He gets me. He made my heart, so He understands every wild thought beating inside there. God remembers my details, my preferences, and my secrets. He knows the song my soul sings and can hum it back to me.

2. He is always available to listen, every second of every day, and He is always interested. I can talk about the same issue twelve times an hour and He will always tilt his head and furrow his brow like it is the first time.

3. He will give me unconditional love and compassion under all circumstances. Who would not want a love affair like that?

I once heard someone say, "There are two constant things God never stops doing; loving us and forgiving us."

Victor Frankl gave me one of the clearest illustrations of how conjuring love in our head can save our literal lives. While he was being starved, beaten, and dehumanized inside Auschwitz, he constantly spoke to his wife inside his head. He credits her with his survival. He said, "Had I known then that my wife was dead, I think I still would have given myself, undisturbed by that knowledge, to the contemplation of her image, and that my mental conversation with her would have been just as vivid and just as satisfying."

Conversation with God can accomplish the same. We can utilize the vivid imagination He granted us to sustain the relationship. We can imagine Him listening, nodding, smiling, answering, and stroking our cheek. Just like Frankl did with his wife.

Through learning and practicing intimacy skills with people we can become better at it with God. How do you grow intimacy between people? One way. Diving deep, discussing the whys and hows of life. When you ask the "who, what, and when" questions, the conversation hovers at the surface. These questions keep you stuck in the small talk. Intimacy lies deeper at the heart level.

Asking the 'why and how' questions grabs the hand of the other and invites them to dive into deep waters with you. "Why did you feel that way?" Or, "How did that make you feel?" This opens up a pocket of intimacy inside the conversation to swim deep inside the vast ocean of other people and explore the coral reef of their heart. If you feel safe enough to enter this heart space with another person, the connection grows rich and satisfying. Weighted matter of the two souls are exchanged and the bond thickens.

Once you become more fluent in conversational intimacy with people, you can use those exact skills with God. Talk to Him. As you tell Him all the whys and hows of your heart, you begin to feel the warm flush of intimacy with Him. He listens and responds gently, with feelings, intuitions, and ideas. He waits patiently inside consciousness for this intimacy. He asked for our circumcised heart more than once inside the Biblical text. That is a pretty graphic and vulnerable request. But He wants nothing less. The fleshy tip of our heart, the part with the most sensitive nerve endings, to touch with His tip to tip.

God wants a real relationship with us. All real relationships require work, compromise, and sacrifice. Listening to the wants and desires of the other and trying our best to deliver. We got lucky! God gave us a five-part book outlining His wants. I try my best to look inside that book to understand the requests God is asking of me, because I so badly want the relationship. Jewish people read a chapter every Saturday; we go through the whole Bible each year. Each go-around I am looking for clues hidden inside the nuances of the text, to tweak things on my end of the relationship. The Torah is one long and mysterious love note.

> *All real relationships require work, compromise, and sacrifice*

In the Bible God paints Himself with the full spectrum of emotions — love, frustration, joy, and anger. Why does He do this? As an invitation to relate to Him in the most natural way we mortal beings know how—inside the *emotional realm*.

When God gave the Torah to Moses on the mountain, God had him set up a boundary at the foot of the mountain, A do-not-cross line. I understood something symbolic from that. We are allowed to play in the emotional field with God, as much as we want, because God constantly describes Himself in emotional terms. The emotional anthropomorphism in the Bible gives implied permission to engage this way. But only Moshe was granted access to the 'head of the mountain'. (Exodus 19:20). From that wording, I inferred that we are not allowed to cross into the mind of God. We can feel all the emotions with God here on earth, but we cannot ascend the mountain to understand His thoughts. Nor should we try to explain His reasons for doing things. We need to stay in the heart-zone, the emotional field, with God during this lifetime. Maybe when we cross back over, we regain access to His thoughts. Maybe that is what Heaven is.

My husband once had the best original thought. He blew me away with this one. He was struggling with some relationships in his life that were dominated by small talk at every single conversation. He could not tolerate another minute of these relationships. He shared this epiphany. "Only after you have established the deeper ties of intimacy with someone, does the mundane conversation become tolerable, even pleasurable. But without the intimacy, you want to kill yourself!" This is so true! True with people and true with God. God asks of us a lot of mundane things. Check your lettuce for bugs, cover your knees and head, do not use electricity on Shabbat.

Once we have established an intimacy with Him, these mundane things become our pleasure. Without intimacy, these minute requests can feel oppressive. After Josh and I developed a beautiful intimacy with each other, I started enjoying talking about the broken washing machine together. Even more miraculous, his loud snoring stopped bothering me as much.

My husband and I were both 21 when we got married and we both came with a lot of emotional baggage.

In those early years of marriage, I feared my husband terribly. Where there is fear, there can be no love. We both were living wildly unconsciously and had no idea how to communicate like people with each other. When you are unaware, you are unaware that you are unaware (Lisa Romano). We attacked each other all the time and like bloodied boxers retreated to our own corners to clean up our wounds. His anger and my fear of his anger did the worst possible thing. It killed any possibility for emotional intimacy. That is the real tragedy that fear plays in any relationship. I had no idea that the words *emotional intimacy* even existed when I was in my twenties, let alone that we were destroying it every time we fought like animals.

Emotional Intimacy is a phrase that I have come to understand as the sharing back and forth of the deepest truths of your heart inside a consistently safe and reliably loving space. Intimacy can only grow along walls of safety. *Safety* is an absolute, non-negotiable prerequisite for intimacy (John Gottman). Fear and Anger suffocate the possibility for emotional intimacy.

So why was the fear of God taught to me as a young child?

Fear is the absolute lowest level to operate *any* relationship from—parent, spouse, or God. In our very early years and most immature times, I remember going to shul on Shabbos morning only because I was afraid Josh would ignore me for the rest of the day if I did not. I am sorry to say, there can be no intimacy in a relationship like that. A relationship where your entire energy is spent keeping your partner's anger at bay. If a fear-based relationship was horrible with my husband, why on earth would I want that with God?

Fear relationships are the worst; they breed resentment, loathing, and distance. That is the real damage done to children who are fed the fear of God in their formative years. That fear of God becomes an indelible blueprint written in permanent marker. Very hard to erase.

During our early years, a loving, trusting intimacy with God has a chance to get hard-wired deep inside our wide-open childhood psyche. Research shows that there is a small window of about seven years to program kids. Children are in a hypnotic, theta-wave brain phase during those early years.

There are only two ways little ones can be programmed to relate to God: Fear or Love. Fear corrupts the innocent system and can take a lifetime to recover the lost intimacy with God that was your birthright. I am still trying to climb myself out of that hole.

Awe of the Creator is where I am trying to go. Awe is the feeling that endlessly fuels Love Affairs. Awe keeps you enchanted and curious. Awe sees the other as separate from you and infinitely capable of unexpected surprises. Awe keeps you wanting more. Awe wants to swim deeper into the mystery. Fear presses you under its thumb.

In an article by Hospice chaplain Kerry Eagan, I read the best description of love. She includes Love with the great Mysteries of life, like Death and God.

"That's really what falling in love is, isn't it? Yearning to know more about a person, the amazement and delight as each layer is peeled back, the realization that you can never get enough of the one you love."

Perhaps the death knell of love is not anger or indifference: it's losing the desire to know more about your partner."

Einstein, with all his scientific brilliance, wanted to know one thing: God's Thoughts. That is awe. To look at the world that God or any person has created and be deeply curious about the thoughts inside that being that generated it.

This is the Love affair I want with God, *endless curiosity.* Curiosity not only keeps you in love, it keeps you from getting old. Why? Because it keeps you open. Open souls are forever young and forever falling in love.

After getting cozy with God inside my consciousness, the only thing left to fear is losing that divine intimacy. So, like I do with my marriage, I check in on my connection every day. Make sure it is still there, that it is Real and it is true.

I never liked hearing that the Jews were the Chosen People. It embarrassed me, made me cringe. It sounded egotistical. I read an explanation from Rav Shlomo Carlebach that reframed those words for me. He said that Jews were chosen to show the world what chosen means and how *every single one of us is Chosen.* We were only called by that name to introduce and illuminate the concept of Chosen. We are all chosen. Every single one of us. I like that much better.

Being Chosen is what every girl wants. To become the first place a man looks to share his heart. The only place a man wants to come home to. To be cherished and treasured above all. How can God choose every single one of us? Because He is God.

More than anything, God wants to experience intimacy with us — the pieces of Himself that broke off, fell to earth, and are now reaching back to Him with the extended hand of our own free will. I can only imagine that God loves being Chosen as much as we do.

We are His reflection. The more we make Him our heart, the more we become His. The greater portion of our inner world we share with Him, the greater portion of His He shares with us. Whatever intimacy we grew here, blossoms like a wildflower (Keren Kayemet L'Olam Habah) on the other side. Because we **chose** Him in a place where we could not see Him. Trusted Him in a place where it made no sense. God's love language is Choice. Every time we choose Him, He chooses us right back. The first two commandments are about Claiming God. Why start out with this and spend two Whole Commandments on it? Because every time you Claim Him, He grabs you, lifts you, twirls you and kisses you.

Imagine that.

Now, imagine the greatest love affair you have ever had. Imagine that person is taken from you at a young age, and you had 50 long years of life ahead of you without them. Imagine the interminable longing and aching of separation. Bottle that feeling. That is exactly how your soul felt when it had to leave God to come here.

Chapter Twelve

Anxiety

"Anxiety lives in the place where God is absent."
— Dr. Zev Zelenko

The *root cause* of all anxiety, if we trace the feeling down to its core, is from temporarily forgetting that you are always connected, protected, and safe inside God. You are cupped, nurtured, and soothed within His gentle hands every second of your breathing life. So, it stands to reason that the *root of all recovery* from anxiety lies in actively reminding ourselves, minute by minute, that He is always right here. Always with us. When we remember to turn our worried mind over to Him, we create that bond with Him. A bond that comes from sharing your deepest, most unspeakable fears with a trusted other. There is a relief that comes from verbalizing the worst possibility out loud, To God.

When we were first married, I paid all the bills. I remember the terror I felt one night when the last check I wrote was for hundreds more than we had in our account. We had three babies at the time and a mortgage. I would normally keep the worry inside; I am not sure why. But that night, a trembling anxious mess, I turned to Josh in bed and choked out what I was feeling. That was the night I learned that when you vent fear out through your mouth, you lessen its hold on you by at least half. The dead weight of worry lightens the moment you release it and let someone else hold it with you.

God can be that someone for you.

Kafka said, "Man cannot live without the continuous belief of something indestructible inside himself." *Let that indestructible thing be your Relationship with God.* Let your Relationship with God be the thing you rely on to call you back from anxiety. Your sturdy safe harbor. Intangible and internal, so no one can touch it.

Anything external and tangible can be destroyed; this is why God asks us to never worship an idol. He is guiding us to a place inside where we can always cling to Him. "Thy Rod and Thy Staff, they comfort me." Imagine yourself holding tight to these from within, as they lead you through this valley of the shadow of death, better known as planet Earth. Imagine yourself a conjoined twin with God, sharing every vital organ with Him.

Rabbi Kaplan said, "Our main link to God is through words." God gave homo sapiens articulated, nuanced speech. No other creature on earth can connect to God with these many words. The other perk that came with speech was the distinct ability to worry ourselves to death. But with our conscious mind at the helm, we can direct each worried word to the ear of God. To find comfort from our fears. We can articulate, in precise words, our specific fears to God and He will hold them with us until we feel better. Eight times in Tehillim, King David asks God to bend His ear — for only one reason. For God to listen to his worries. David understood this secret. When we use our capacity for speech to tell Him our fears, we give God the opportunity to come comfort us.

Martha Beck had a great insight about worrying. "People blossom when we love them, not when we worry about them."

Worrying only adds more worry to a big boiling pot of worry. Worrying feels like when you start losing a game of Tetris. The worried thoughts keep stacking, compounding bricks of worry until we are overtaken and fully frazzled. Worrying solves nothing.

Worrying about your kids, especially in front of your kids, does not help them, it only teaches them your specific style and technique of worry. When you find yourself worrying about a loved one, flip the emotion to love. If your intention is to help them, your love will help them infinitely more than your worry ever could. Let everyone in your atmosphere experience you as a peaceful presence. That is the best way to help anxious people.

PRAYER

Any feeling or word offered towards God from inside your consciousness is prayer. The Kotzker Rebbe said, "Be alert, and be brief, even when you pray."

Moshe Rabbeinu knew this. When his sister Miriam was sick, he said five short words. *"El Na, Refah Na La." Please God, Please Heal Her.* So simple. So effective. Two of those five words were "Please." His prayer emerged from a reservoir of calm trust in the **established relationship**. A prayer that was simply a continuation of the conversation.

You can cut a clear path to the face of God with simple prayer.

Many short-burst prayers become reflex through repetition. Prayers that jump out of your consciousness all on their own. Knee-jerk prayers.

> I TRUST YOU
> THANK YOU
> I NEED YOU
> BE WITH ME
> HELP ME
> I LOVE YOU

We all get triggered by the small and big trials of life. Someone blocked your driveway, or you stubbed your toe, or your boyfriend broke your heart, or your printer ran out of ink, or you miss your mom who died five years ago. Reflexively remembering one of these mini prayers can bounce us back from the dark side pretty quickly. They catch us by the collar as we are about to fall backwards down the rabbit hole.

These mini prayers are like a labeled panel of circuit breakers. They quickly flip energy back to your soul. These short bursts of prayer instantly convert fear back to gratitude, loneliness back to comfort, ego back to humility, heartbreak back to trust.

My introduction to prayer was rough. At 6-years-old, I was given a siddur in school. Taught the right words to say and the rules that go with them. When to stand, when to sit, when to bow. I was told by hovering Rabbis to hold my finger on the place and say the words clearly.

There was one tiny thing they left out — that this was my sweet and precious time to commune with God. Making sure to pronounce all the words correctly is important, I am sure. But I cannot remember hearing that this was the chance to connect my heart to the Creator's.

> *We all get triggered by the small and big trials of life*

It is heartbreaking to give a small child instructions for prayer tucked inside guilt and perfectionism. It misses the whole point.

I was in JFK airport a few years ago, sitting at the gate, waiting for my flight. There was a slender Muslim woman kneeling on a small rug alongside the glass wall of windows that looks out onto the tarmac. She looked immersed and radiant with her covered head and closed eyes. I was having a serious staring problem. The sight of her devotion and concentration swirled up a cacophony of emotions inside my Jewish heart. *Jealous* at the sight of her tight relationship with Allah. *Guilty* for not being a good Jew who prays three times a day (she does this 5 times a day?). *Inspired* by her discipline and devotion. *Awed* by her lack of embarrassment. Why do I care that people will think I am a weirdo mumbling to herself in public? The emotions were real.

According to the rules of the Jews, women are more innately spiritual and do not have to pray the same structured way that men do, but I still feel bad that I do not. I take five minutes most mornings to rattle off my blessings. This dampens the guilt and makes me feel tethered to my day. But my biggest reprieve from prayer-guilt is staying in constant conversation with God. Talking to Him all day long is my biggest sanity-keeper, my reservoir of joyfulness, playfulness, and ease. I think this type of impromptu prayer counts for more than we were taught. USE ME, is another favorite mini-prayer. I chant this inside my heart from when I park my car all the way to the front door of my office, a block and a half of prayer. Use me for good. Use me to help people heal. Use me so that other people feel You through my hands.

Use me so that everyone who sits in my chair will feel better just from having been near me. Use me with perfect ease so it does not require more effort than feeling love in my heart. (I do not want to go home depleted). Dentists have a special advantage. When we work on people, their heads are right near our hearts; the waves of love do not have far to travel.

Prayer is a confidential communication with God. It can be as specific and weird as you want it to be. Only you and He know the strange stuff you said. Most of the time we are not privy to the effect our prayer has. We offer it up and let it go. We can only hope our words line up with God's will and have some sway on events. But sometimes we are given a gift. A nod from God.

Gilad Schalit was an Israeli soldier held captive by Palestinian terrorists for over five years. He was always somewhere in my prayers. In the news, there had been rumors circulating of his release. On Friday evening of October 14, 2011, I stood quietly in front of my Shabbat candles. With my face cupped inside my hands, a strangely specific prayer came to my lips. One that only God heard me say. I asked God, "Let this be the last Friday night that I pray for the release of Gilad Schalit. Let him come home safely this week."

No other captive had ever been returned alive by the Palestinians. Would he be murdered like Daniel Pearl and Nachshon Wachsman? The unfolding events were terrifyingly uncertain. Days later, we all held our collective breath as we watched in wide-eyed disbelief footage of a starved and frail Gilad Schalit stumble down the plane hatch, salute, and embrace Bibi on the tarmac.

Our boy was delivered back home safely. A palpable miracle. Thank God that I was totally alone as I watched this on my phone. I did not have to hold back one ounce of my most twisted, ugly face cry. I let it run its full glory. I allowed relief, gratitude, and amazement come through every muscle of my face.

It did not dawn on me until later that day that Gilad returned safely in the time span, I had casually mentioned to God. International news morphed into something deeply personal. Now, I know it was not only my prayer that made it happen. But to have my words correlate to the timeline of events in the world is something more than transcendent. The timing and wording of my will lined up with the will of heaven. The edges all lined up in a neat stack. The synchronicity took my breath away. Heaven always registers every word of every prayer, and once in a while, lets you know.

When a prayer I have been holding in my heart for a LONG time finally comes through, it excites all the electrons in my body. An exhilarating blend of gratitude and relief, disbelief and humility, all jump together and swirl around.

My sister Dina had been dating for 7 years, which in Jewish years equals 47. Fed up with the system, we drove together to a remote and holy gravesite in Israel to pray for her to find her man. The Sephardic man whose dead mother left him in charge over there handed Dina candlesticks to use every Friday night to help her situation. She shook her head and told him no. Single girls do not usually light candles on Friday night and she did not want to take on the extra responsibility. I grabbed those candlesticks from his hands and said, "I'll do it!" I lit those candlesticks every week.

I closed my eyes and imagined myself handing them over to her after she got married. I held that visual prayer in my imagination every week for two years.

Then she met Alon. The man that she had manifested through a personal prayer of her own. She asked God to meet him naturally. No more blind dates, no more set-ups, and no more resumes. She bravely left 'the system' and put her fate in God's hands. I told her this was a crazy and reckless move. She did not listen to me. She trusted and prayed.

God became their personal and divine matchmaker at a hotel on Passover in Orlando, Florida. After her wedding, when everything settled down, I finally had my chance to hand over the candlesticks. She looked at me and said, "I don't really like them." Not exactly how I pictured it going down. But then I remembered a prettier set of crystal candlesticks from Marshall's that I had inside my drawer. I handed those to her, and she has been using them ever since.

When a personal prayer gets answered, you can feel God blowing His breath into the nooks and crannies of your mind and down your spine.

Why does an answered prayer feel so good? Your will was in alignment with His will. Your human plan vibed with God's Divine plan. That is the most glorious sensation on earth.

Original candlesticks from the

Graveside of Rabbi Yonatan Ben Uziel

My acceptance of His infinite wisdom and timing helps me stop micromanaging the beautiful way God wants to bless my life. When I am open to His will, he is open to mine. When I honor His will, He honors mine. If I am listening for His, He is listening for mine. It is a reciprocal energy that starts within us. When I align myself with His will by saying, 'God, I trust that the plan you have for my life is good." This feeling of trust fast- tracks my vibration up to the **creation frequency range** where God's will and my will can mingle freely and work together. When my prayers become infused with humility and trust: *"God, You know better and I trust you."* God loves to meet me inside that vibrational space and collaborate with whatever is brewing inside my heart.

TRUST

I TRUST YOU.

I would like to plunge a little deeper into this mini prayer. Saying *I TRUST YOU* to God, from inside my heart is very powerful. It feels like an industrial-strength bug zapper. Whenever an anxious, questioning, or doubting thought flies around my head, the moment I catch the thought, trap it, and zap it with these three words, the offending thought is immediately neutralized.

Connection is a three-beverage cocktail. Trust, Vulnerability, and Intimacy (TVI) get shaken together. They mix very well and enhance each other.

Trust has your back in all situations

Vulnerability tells you all its embarrassing secrets

Intimacy shows you its naked soul

Trust must come first. Once you trust someone, because you saw they have your back, you can drop your guard and let yourself be **vulnerable**. Once you are vulnerable and share the secrets of your heart safely, your soul opens up a space for naked **intimacy** with them. Once you are successfully vulnerable and intimate with someone, the trust gets reinforced. All three fortify each other. These three words are so energetically similar they can almost be used interchangeably. They are tied together loosely in a bundle. One of these emotions cannot flourish inside a relationship all by itself. You need all three to play off each other. They are the emotional trifecta we crave inside our closest relationships. TVI is the only real cure for addiction and loneliness.

When these emotions are cultivated inside relationships with people, their substance solidifies inside your consciousness. A tangible TVI can be grasped by the hands of your heart and circulated upward, towards their ultimate destination: Total Surrender to God. You cultivate these three emotions with people in order to experience them with God. People are the practice.

Trust, Vulnerability and Intimacy (TVI) escort you all the way to Surrender. If you climb your heart into the realm of Surrender you will discover a land of peace, joy, ease, and healing of all heartbreak. *The Land of Surrender is a place where you resist nothing and accept everything.* But you must do the work of the climb, the TVI. Once you get there, you will look back at the struggles that got you there, and you will thank them. They pushed your butt up the ladder.

A friend I grew up with in Scranton lost a newborn baby boy to SIDS. I remember the terrifying elevator ride up to her apartment in Brooklyn, to pay the worst kind of shiva call. I also remember the comforting words she said to me that day. "My baby is in a place where this makes sense." This was my first experience of falling into the visceral comfort of trusting God.

It all starts with Trust. When you clear a space for unconditional trust inside a relationship, you also give vulnerability and intimacy room to grow. There is no greater force that bonds a relationship than trust. Trust feels like letting go and dropping into the sturdy, waiting arms of another. Resting the soft animal of your body (Mary Oliver) into their cupped hands. This feels good with people and even more so with God.

How is trust generated between beings? By gently placing your fate in the hands of another with the calm assumption that they only want the best for you, and they will do everything in their power to deliver it. Think of a band of brothers in the army. Their lifelong camaraderie was forged by placing life and death in each other's hands. Those guys have a palpable level of trust born from being mortally vulnerable together. An intimacy born from knowing they have each other's back in the most profound way. If you can generate this kind of unshakeable surrender with God, you will feel safe and protected all the time.

There are people who trust everyone (me) and people who trust no one. There has to be a happy medium in there somewhere. When I live in the present moment and listen to the whisper of my intuition (soul), I learn how to weed out the creeps. When I do confer my trust, the universe tends to deliver people worthy of my trust. If I become suspicious of everyone, more people worthy of my suspicion come knocking at my door.

I tend to get what I expect. I have seen in my life that by placing the treasured energy of trust into the hands of someone who feels right, more often than not, they meet me there.

In my dental office, inside the privacy of my treatment room, I sit on my rolling chair and deliver annoying news all day. You have six cavities. You need a root canal. This tooth has to come out. Then I launch into my dental blabber. The hows and whys and different treatment options available. There are certain holy individuals, I do not know where they come from or how they got here, who glance at me casually in the eye and say the most wonderful thing anyone could ever say to their dentist: "I trust you; do whatever needs to be done."

I immediately feel a warm flush of affection rise up. I shut up. This rare person unwittingly uttered the magic words to me, and now they have my heart forever. And the best care. And the best price. If someone needles me with questions or doubts me or blames me, that produces the exact opposite energy within me and ends up working against them. They will receive my care from a more distant and reserved place. It will be good; it just will not be the same.

(Side note: the worst thing to say to a dentist: "It didn't hurt until you touched it." No one enjoys the subtle energy of blame. Not even God.)

What this precious patient conveyed to me inside those three tiny words is that they know unequivocally that I want the best for them. I do not have to waste another syllable on explanation. They trust me! These three words tell me they understand that I will not factor anything selfish into the equation, I will simply do the right thing.

Their trust has elevated my motivation and intentions to the highest level possible. They freed me to fix their teeth joyfully, without the uncomfortable insinuation of ulterior motive that over-questioning often generates. Trust always has a way of making my work extra beautiful.

Two or three questions are fine. Inquiring minds want to know. But patients who barrage me with one hundred questions do not understand the distrust they are conveying. It makes the energy in the room feel adversarial. Which muddles up my ability to operate from the highest version of myself. I get distracted by what they think of me and how to explain it right, rather than just getting down to the beautiful business of fixing teeth.

I want to be that kind of dental patient with God. To whisper an, 'I trust you' from my heart every single moment of the day. Give Him the luxurious space to do His work joyfully without all my questions annoying the crap out of Him. To halt my own micromanaging and instead say with perfect ease, "I trust you," and feel the commensurate measure of appreciation rise up from God to meet me.

The light of a single *I trust you* has the power to dispel a hundred dark *whys*.

Why did my tooth decay?

Why do I need a crown instead of a filling?

Why do I need to get numb?

People have every right to ask these questions, and I will answer every single one. But, when they surrender their whys into my care and my hands they will walk out with my best work. Because, damn, they trusted me. These patients remind me of the best way to trust God — minimal questions. I know He is got me, let Him work. I want God to feel that beautiful release.

If you keep building your trust muscle, you will end up with Might. Rabbi Akiva was caught by the Romans teaching Torah in a time when it was forbidden. He was sentenced to the most horrible death. The Romans flayed his flesh with iron combs in a public arena. During the brutality, it was witnessed by his students that he smiled and said Shema. How was this even possible? What could have been going through his mind?

Rabbi Akiva told his students that his whole life he feared he would not be able to serve God with all his Might, as the Shema asks of us. He was not even sure what the word Might meant, until that moment. Maybe he smiled because he understood this as his opportunity to attain the lofty level of Might. Might cannot be pre-planned; it is a game-time reflex. Might is the result of cumulative conditioning of Trust a person has been cultivating his whole life, To be able to call to Hashem in calm prayer instead of panic from within the crisis.

At a time of grave distraction, when no one would blame Rabbi Akiva for forgetting to call out to God, he was mortally proud that he was able to summon Might over fear. *He came through for himself.* The satisfaction of remembering to reach for intimacy with God during the height of physical pain was euphoric; it was Might. All he could bring himself to do in that Olympic Moment of might was smile.

Mary Neal did it too. When she was pinned to her kayak, submerged under a waterfall of hydraulic pressure, all she remembers saying was, "Your will, not mine..." What a victory of Might.

I want to Trust God during the following:

When things make no sense.

When I am suffering.

When people I love are suffering.

When I think things should have been different.

When I regret mistakes that I have made.

When a dream I long for seems far away.

One heartfelt "*I Trust You*" can soothe all of the above.

I once heard R' Gabriel Sassoon, who lost seven young children in a house fire, say something really practical about the way he Surrenders to God. He said, "Sometimes I need to surrender every five minutes." Wow. That was gold to me. Surrender is *constant work,* never one and done. The Trusting of God's will over your own, over and over again, every single time the grief creeps back in.

My biggest "*I Trust You*" belongs to the Holocaust. Eli Wiesel got it right when he said that the Holocaust must forever remain a question mark. Any attempt to explain the Holocaust is mortally insulting to the dead and a disgrace to the living. Wiesel is warning that it is dangerous territory to enter the mind of God. Yellow tape: Do not cross. You will confuse yourself and others.

Our only choice with the Holocaust is to live with the Why stuck in our throat until we get back to the other side. We can neutralize every "*why*" that rises from our mind with an "*I Trust You*" that rises from our heart. The sickening brutality and cold-organized savagery of the Nazis will never make sense, which makes it one of history's greatest opportunities for Trust.

On my trip to Poland in the winter of 2017, we visited all the horrendous places. The tour guide told our group the most gruesome stories. Of babies being torn in half, of pregnant bellies being sliced open, of children put into bags, pummeled and buried alive. We heard the eye-witness accounts at the hallowed ground where they happened. I am someone who has a hard time recovering after watching the news at night. In Poland, the only thing that soothed the frayed edges of my soul at night would be to rock myself to sleep with *I Trust You* on a repeat loop in my mind. It was the only way through.

I Trust that You know what You are doing.

I Trust that this all makes sense on the other side.

I Trust that this is a microscopic sliver of a bigger picture that is obscured from view in order to grant us the singular opportunity to Trust You.

Our Ancestors made many colossal mistakes stemming from a lack of Trust in God. God wants us to Trust Him when we are being hunted and pursued (jumping into the Red Sea), when dates do not add up (the Golden calf), when we are hungry and frustrated (with only manna to eat). When we get a bad report (The Spies). He wants us to Trust Him through the untrustable. Let the flush of fear pass through you then reach in deeper for the trust. Because once the storm passes, the opportunity for trust goes with it.

An "I Trust You" eked out within hardship does the work of a thousand "I Trust You's" said calmly during the good times. Looking upward inside the eye of the storm with Trust zooms you right up to the face of God. You and He will always remember the intimacy that Moment of Might held.

In the summer of 2013, my son's good friend Aaron was killed in a tragic boating accident. Aaron was a special soul. I miss him all the time. His unique energy and scratchy voice. He was just ten years old and already had a following. At the funeral, the Rabbi who spoke described the scene at Aaron's bedside. His father sang him the songs they always sang together on Friday night at the Shabbat table. This was how Aaron passed from this world, with his father singing to him. That is Trust in the eye of the storm. That is Might. This must be a man who practices his trust in God so regularly that inside the worst moment of his life, it kicked in like a reflex.

I have missed many opportunities for Might by being afraid instead of trusting. But there was one time I did not. When I was 29 years old, my in-laws took my family away to a hotel for Rosh Hashana and my legs started to feel weird and tingle the first night we got there. By the time we got home two days later, I was numb from the waist down. I had motor function, just no sensory. My legs felt like clumps. I was terrified. I did not tell anyone.

One especially terrified night, I stood up from the couch and spontaneously walked over to the bookshelf in my living room. I took a siddur off the shelf and started praying some standard prayers. I felt something wonderful come over me. A wave of gratitude rolled into my heart. The fear that had been consuming me vanished. My 29-year-old heart somehow remembered to find a spark of trust inside the paralyzing fear. I remember the exact words that came to me: "Thank you for the healthy life I had until now; I am so grateful. Whatever happens next will be fine."

This was a real turning point for me. A moment of Might. It matured my relationship with God. I was learning the mysterious alchemy of Gratitude. How it can flip anxiety and worry into trust and calm. That gratitude can make you a vessel worthy of receiving comfort from above. Most of all, that I hold the capacity to modulate and regulate my own emotions in order to Connect.

The highest level our soul can reach is to walk comfortably through the chaos of life. To be loose and Trust that Heaven is the place of answers. The Shimmering Clarity that comes to retrieve your soul will be the most alluring angel of heaven. She will be the reason you recognize the place.

Chapter Thirteen

Free Will

Born stupid is another way to say it. At birth we are wiped clean, erased, plunged in amnesia. Remember the poor folk in Men in Black who accidentally saw too much? They got the red light flashed in their eyes. Yes, that is us. *All of us have* no idea *WHERE we came from, WHO we are, or WHAT we are doing here*. We do not have any language at birth, even if we did remember. We need to relearn *everything*. It turns out that there is one basic prerequisite for life on earth:
complete and total amnesia.

Amnesia just so happens to be the same prerequisite for choosing God. For some reason (a reason none of us can remember), choosing God must be done from a place of total stupidity for it to be worth something. Use your stupidity wisely. You will not be stupid forever. Turns out, this mammoth volume of free will (stupidity) is the exact amount needed to advance the entire wheel of creation. *Earthlings (I think) are the stupidest beings in all the Universe; we therefore wield the most influence over planetary ascension*. The entire cosmos is relying on our stupidity, er... ability to choose hope over despair, kindness over cruelty — to actually get us somewhere. To hurtle us towards 5-D consciousness (aka Mashiach). To lift our planet out of FEAR and into the bandwidth of LOVE.

Whenever I played hide and seek as a kid, if the seeker took more than five minutes to find me, I got annoyed and gave up hiding. But when you love the person seeking you, you give them as long as they need to find you. So they can feel the accomplishment of the find. So they can feel good about winning the game. Some poor people do not even know there's a game going on. God is extra patient with those.

The moment God becomes obvious to us on the other side, our free will poof! evaporates. Free will exists only inside the frank stupidity of this realm. Free will is the reason we came here. To choose Him from this place of darkness and confusion and have a chance to earn the relationship all on our own. That is the point of the game. I think. I do not really remember.

Free will exists in four domains:

Thought
Speech
Action
Reaction

High level players understand that free will revolves around these four activities — what we think, say, do, and refrain from doing. We exercise our free will inside these four different arenas. Free will is our birthright. We claim it by propping our runner's foot on the starting block of free will — thoughts of the mind.

Free will of Thought. Our thoughts belong to us, no one else. You can think about any situation in any way you want. Spin your thoughts around until they bring you peace. Until they spiral you right up to God's face. Do not let your thoughts think you into oblivion. Grab the wheel and steer those bad boys in the right direction. Sometimes it is the hardest thing to do.

Question: The Polish people who risked their lives to hide Jews from the Nazis, or the Palestinians that came to love Israelis, how were they so drastically different from the world around them?

Answer: They exercised their Free Will of Thought in the direction of love and tolerance. They were outliers who not only brazenly stepped outside the collective hate mindset, they jumped to step three and *acted* fiercely on those brave thoughts.

The most elevated way to use our gift of Free Will of Thought (FWOT) is to handpick thoughts geared towards intimacy with God. Towards trusting Him. Towards connecting to Him. Towards adoring Him and adoring His creations. Towards thanking Him. Towards thinking happy and hopeful things. This habit of grooming your thoughts is every day.

Free will in speech. God showed us how He created His world: He used *words*. Word and world are only one skinny letter apart! The soul inside us that is One with God carries this verbal creative power, too. Every word out of our mouth has creative force. Never let a word escape your lips that you do not want to show up on your hips. Never call yourself bald, fat, old, or ugly. Speak beauty and wealth onto your life and onto your loved ones, every time. A new neighbor was telling me all about the problems she was having with the new house. She said, out loud, to me, "I must be cursed." As the words left her mouth, I felt a slow motion...noooo... come over me. I wish I could have rewound the tape and folded those words back into her mouth. A short time later her $5,000 outdoor air conditioning unit got stolen, for the *second* time.

Free will in action. That one is obvious. Either cut the grass or do not, your choice. But whatever action you choose to do, put the full force of free will behind it. Let the intention behind any action be to serve the Creator and humanity. So, whatever you are physically doing can generate the most impact. So it can ripple.

Free will in reaction. This comes after you realize that you can actually decide the way you want to react. Take the moment and regroup. Let the "whoosh" pass and reach for your higher self to react more calmly. Observe your first insane consciousness and reach for the second calmer one. (Terry Real). Brush your thoughts until they are trained in the direction of peace and optimism. This gives you the best chance to exercise your Free Will in reaction properly, and not lose your mind. Train your lungs to take a deep breath before you say even one word.

You are the co-creator of your life with God.

> 'Ha'Yotzer Yachad Libam'. (Psalms 33:15)
> God Creates How?
> *Together with our hearts.*

He is a loving partner to all we do, even more so when we include Him in the process. Mix your creative juices with His. Let your heart and mind gently intermingle with God's plan for your life. Ask for anything you want and let it all be His decision after that. Trust that He will protect you from the things that are not good for you.

Do life on purpose: think on purpose, speak on purpose, act on purpose, react on purpose, use your imagination on purpose.

> *You are the co-creator of your life with God*

The changes come! There is usually a lag time, so be careful not to let them slip past you unnoticed. Stand back and take pleasure in what you partnered with God to create. My children, my office, my marriage, this book were all tiny dreams in my mind. They are here now. My dreams have strong arms and sturdy legs. I shake my head in deep humility for the brick and mortar, the flesh and blood. I was not even half as awake as I am now when I thought these dreams into existence.

REFLECTION

You and I and the UPS delivery guy are all God's **reflection**. God Himself called us this interesting noun. God gave every soul infinite potential to reflect the multi-faceted prisms His Crystalline Character holds. The Hebrew word, *Midah,* can mean two different things: a measurement or a personality trait. The conventional translation for the biblical expression, "*Midah K'neged Midah,*" is similar to the concept of Karma. The phrase translates as punishment meted out by God "measure for measure." An eye for an eye.

I prefer to plug the other translation of the word Midah into *Midah K'neged Midah.* God will reward us "character trait for character trait." Whatever trait we reflect up to Him, He will reflect it back down to us (AM).

God spelled out His Character Traits clearly in the Bible, with the Thirteen Attributes. When we match our character traits (our Midot) to reflect His Thirteen Attributes, we fit our essence more seamlessly inside His. We become closer reflections. We oscillate and vibrate on the same Divine wavelength.

What is the advantage in matching God's vibe? Our creative power gets amplified, and we manifest more quickly.

God delineates His character with thirteen different forms of kindness, forgiveness, compassion, and truth. Emulating these traits are the work that constitutes an awakened life. Whichever of these character traits we work hard to develop become ours to keep. They go back with us to the other side. Character becomes the shape of our soul. It is the work your soul came down here to accomplish. Not Ego. Not pride. Not credit-seeking. Not manipulation. Not score keeping. Just authentic character development, for its own sake.

When my oldest daughter was in middle school, a page in her binder sat open on the dining room table. It had colorful balloon letters that jumped off the page at me. It said, "All you have is your Character," Rabbi Yisroel Salanter.

This was a stand-still moment. A moment that caught my soul. The Rabbis knew then what I only begin to understand today, that *character is everything*. My kids teach me about character all the time. They astound me. When my oldest daughter was 15, she met a boy at a Bar Mitzvah weekend. He started calling and texting her. Innocent "Will you be my girlfriend" kind of stuff. She liked him. We called him "boy" and giggled about it together. After a few days, she asked him if his parents knew he was talking to a girl. He said no. She said she could not continue talking to him if they did not know about it and she stopped, cold turkey. She taught me about unwavering integrity and moral fortitude. Innate teenage integrity.

My other daughter was in sleepaway camp, and she witnessed a bee crawl into the ear of a friend while they were swimming. She ran with her to tell the counselors. No adult believed them. (Kids are the most disbelieved and disregarded population). My daughter did not relent until one of the nurses finally looked inside with a flashlight and saw the bee. Innate Loyalty and Devotion.

My son has been friends with kids in his class with special needs ever since he was in first grade. His teacher back then told me how sweet it was of him. I knew immediately that he was not going out of his way to be nice, he genuinely does not see anything wrong with them. Innate Acceptance and Inclusion.

Whenever I was sad and crying in my room, my youngest son, at six years old, would come find me and silently stroke my arm. Innate Empathy and Compassion.

Faith
Gratitude
Trust
Kindness
Forgiveness
Surrender
Truth
Loyalty
Integrity
Compassion
Empathy

This is the short list of ingredients that make up character; the things our soul strives to acquire for itself on this short trip. The things that only God Himself can discern their level of sincerity. The benchmark of character change comes when doing wrong feels too icky. As Brene Brown said, "When it feels too uncomfortable to go back." You know you have arrived somewhere when judging, gossiping, lying, or holding a grudge just feels too gross and intolerable to your soul. Your soul is beginning to match the soul of God.

My oldest daughter went to Israel at 18 years old. She told me that she and a group of her friends were approached by a needy woman asking for money. She said that she was the only one who stepped aside and gave this woman something. The woman proceeded to bestow on her a hundred blessings. My daughter told me something that made me feel like for all the mistakes I have made with my kids, I did one thing right. She told me that when she gave the woman money, *she felt like me*. If this is the exuberance God feels when He sees us trying to be like Him, it is the best gift we could ever give Him.

KINDNESS

Kindness is the great equalizer; it makes you see everyone as human.

Kindness makes your soul shimmering and iridescent to all other souls.

I usually do not cry when something is sad. I used to try to cry to conform to social norms. But I will not fake it anymore. I have no trouble empathizing with people, I just cannot bring myself to

> *Kindness is the great equalizer; it makes you see everyone as human*

Cry at sadness. The only consistent thing that makes me well up is — kindness. Especially large-scale kindness. When Humanity comes together in kindness, the huge lump that swells in my throat will not even let me speak. Kindness always makes me cry.

Every year on 9/11, I watch the 12-minute YouTube video called The Boatlift. Without any planning or coordination, after a panicked call went out from the coast guard, hundreds of regular people with boats of all sizes converged on lower Manhattan and rescued over half a million frantic people. The captured image of all the boats spontaneously racing towards one destination, coming together in kindness, chokes me up every time,

"The great boatlift of 9/11 became the largest sea evacuation in history. Larger than the evacuation of Dunkirk in WWII, where 339,000 British and French soldiers were rescued over the course of 9 days. On 9/11 nearly 500,000 civilians were rescued from Manhattan by boat...it took less than 9 hours."

This mass convergence for the sake of kindness eliminated the need for weeks of meeting, planning, strategizing, debating, and executing. This rescue happened organically, spontaneously, and effortlessly, not one argument or accident. God's alignment was all over the place. That is the power of acting purely for the sake of Heaven; the Force of God gets behind it. God sends out his best invisible coordinators.

I was at a Tony Robbins course with my husband, and it was a Saturday. It was 2pm and I was getting HUNGRY. We had no food or money on us, because it was Shabbos. I went to the concession counter to see if I could buy a snack using my memorized credit card number. The cashier said no.

I asked if she could check with a manager. She said no. Defeated, I started to turn and walk away. A pretty girl with long brown hair and big blue eyes was standing behind me in line watching the whole thing. She came up to me gently and asked me in her sweet voice if there was something she could do to help. I sheepishly explained my situation. She swiftly stepped up to the counter, grabbed my abandoned potato chips and M&M's and paid for them. She handed them to me smiling. Oh crap. I felt the avalanche coming. I could hardly choke out a thank you before the lip-quivering began. Ask my husband. I ran to the nearest corner and cried for ten minutes. Her unsolicited kindness pressed that cry button in my soul. Morgan was her name. I will never forget her.

In the Bible, when Eliezer went out in search of a mate for Isaac, he looked for one thing. He looked for the woman who would not only offer him a drink but would also offer one to his camels. Why would this set her apart? Perhaps he understood that someone who extends kindness to animals is looking for no credit other than the sincere feeling of helping another creature.

Kindness is a remedy. It heals in both directions: the giver and the receiver. The Receiver feels like someone saw them and cared. The Giver gets lifted out of whatever misery they may be experiencing at the moment. Kindness does something magical. It flips the lens. It turns our attention outward; it scans the room looking for ways to help, and in doing so heals the sadness inside. The reward of giving kindness is the healing it gives to you. Kindness replaces your own misery with a specific euphoria called "the Helper's High." When I give a homeless person along the Van Wyck a $20 bill, the feeling it buys me is worth ten times that, easily. Who wouldn't pay for that drug?

However, this is where I sometimes get in trouble. Because Kindness has one huge requirement: Boundaries.

BOUNDARIES

No one was meant to give it all away: Not financially, not emotionally, not physically, not spiritually. This was a hard lesson for me. Giving away money used to be a way for me to accomplish two important things:

1. Alleviate the guilt I felt for my success.

2. Ease the distress I felt at seeing someone else suffering financially.

I would pay anything to shut those uncomfortable feelings down. But after a while, the giving stopped feeling good. I realized that I was swapping one set of negative emotions for another. Guilt and distress were being replaced with resentment and avoidance. My guilt-giving landed me inside a bottomless pit of resentment. I needed something to set myself right again. I needed boundaries. Brene Brown gave me the easiest guideline for creating a boundary.

"What is okay and what is not okay for you."

I use her definition all day long to check if my boundaries are intact. Simple as that. Boundaries are the sturdy gate guarding your sanity and emotional well-being. You get to build them, change them, and take them down as you see fit. They should not be too thick or too thin. They should be flexible enough to allow you to love everyone without getting hurt and without hurting others.

Boundaries are always in flux. *Your* boundaries look different than *mine* do a. And mine look different on Friday than they did on Monday. They are always changing in shape and thickness depending on who or what you are dealing with. A narcissist requires a thick wall. A puppy does not. As you evolve and become more internally confident and secure, your needs for personal safety change. You can constantly shift your boundaries to accommodate your new position.

God created the world with boundaries. Sky and earth. Land and sea. Boundaries delineate the external world for us. A house with no walls, a pool with no sides, a body with no skin, none of that works. Pictures look better inside a frame. If we do not see where the ocean begins and ends, we will always be drowning. We use boundaries to put a frame around our soul. Boundaries allow our soul to safely navigate this world. Do you want to build for your soul a concrete barrier or a flexible one? Do you want your soul to be able to breathe and not be smothered by too many boundaries?

If you have done the daily work of strengthening your soul through a trusting relationship with God, your soul becomes less emotionally affected by its environment. Your soul will then require fewer boundaries. A soul with less boundaries has a HUGE perk. *It is more open and has more access to the joy and divine connection all around us.* You still need to establish boundaries as they feel necessary. A soul with zero boundaries cannot survive in this world.

Boundaries tell us where we end, and the next person begins. As Terry Real says, boundaries are to our psyche what skin is to our body. Boundaries release us from feeling overly responsible for other people. Not everything is our problem to fix. I can trust the capable soul of the next person to fix its own problems. It is made of the same stuff as mine. This is incredibly liberating for me. I love to fix problems; I am like a man that way. When I hear people complaining, I am already mapping out a way to save them.

I have come to realize that the only type of fixing that endures is when people fix their *own* lives. Anything I do for them will only be a temporary patch. Sometimes doing *nothing* is the most efficient way of helping them. People need to *save themselves* for the saving to actually work. Not rescuing everyone is an important boundary, my particular soul needed in order to enjoy this life. Boundaries require us to pay close attention internally to that split second when your pinky toe crosses one inch over into *not okay* territory.

There is a skinny, sweet man who washes cars right outside of my office. He asked me a bunch of times if he could wash mine. I smiled, *no thanks*, each time. Then one day he asked if I could help him out with some money instead. I said, *okay*, and handed him a twenty. He proceeded to ask me every week thereafter if he could 'borrow' $20. He would either tap on the window where I sit at my desk and startle me (I started closing the shade), or he would leave a handwritten post-it note with my office manager asking for the money. The mounting dread I felt each time I saw him was suffocating.

My office manager could not take it anymore either. If I saw him on the street, I would hide. When I could not take it anymore.

I decided to take baby steps towards liberation. I finally got up the nerve to ask him to stop knocking on my window. Next, in very clear and firm language, I asked him to come only on the first Monday of every month to collect his $20. My assistant helped me do this. Interestingly, he abides very well by this new boundary. Almost as if he feels better, too. I know I feel better. I do not loathe him or myself anymore.

As I write this, I realize how obvious this was. Of course, I could put up that simple boundary. Duh. The internal process was rough, though. I thought I was being a bad person if I did not give him money each time he asked. I was ignoring the yucky feeling mounting in me. I was not letting it speak. I was stuck in a false-guilt-mode of what I should be *doing* instead of accepting what I was actually *feeling*. Once I accepted that this is me, this is what I am feeling right now, once I heeded the call of the boundary, the physical steps I needed to take became crystal clear.

When my true feelings are desperately trying to flag me down and I ignore them, I am betraying myself. Emotions are the flashing lights of my soul, trying desperately to get a message up to my brain. Part of my soul gets suffocated each time I suppress an emotion, as if I am holding a hand over my soul's mouth. My soul wrestles and resists and responds with a stronger emotion until I finally listen. Annoyance becomes frustration becomes rage.

Kindness without boundaries will eat you alive. The boundaryless act of kindness will carry dread inside it. This energy feels icky to both the giver and to the receiver. We all can sense when it has been someone's pleasure to help and when it has not.

Another story of boundaries.

In my office, we started a tradition of ordering lunch every Thursday. It was my treat. Gradually, we started ordering from the same place every single week. A place that I do not particularly love. I knew from my feelings that it could not continue like this. There was a leak in my boat and water was filling up fast. Unresolved boundary violations grow stronger over time. Emotional intensity builds along that timeline. You start out mildly annoyed and slowly climb your way to raging lunatic. The bigger the emotion — the longer you have let the situation go on. Feeling *taken advantage of* is an unresolved boundary violation that grew stronger over time.

I sat alone at my desk and let all the emotions about this lunch situation flurry around inside me. I asked them what they needed and how we could fix this. I dropped my resistance and became calm and curious instead. Solutions started bubbling up. Why not start a rotation?

Why not write down a list of four local places, one for each Thursday of the month? I jotted down the list and gave it to the person in charge. I was able to communicate my plan in a calm, centered voice, not apologetic, angry or weak. The boundary breach was repaired. The emotions settled back down – their job was done, boundary restored.

I sat back down to write, after taking a 2-week break to celebrate the Jewish holidays. I found this topic where I had left off and I laughed. I laughed at the synchronicity of life. During the break, I was given another huge opportunity to repair another ongoing boundary violation. A boundary breach that I allowed to go on for way too long. I had wandered deep into the dark forest of *taken advantage*.

There was a patient, a family friend, who only came to see me when she had a dental emergency. She always pushed me to see her that day. Well, this time, I could not offer her an appointment until the next day. The next day came, and she did not show up. I texted her to find out why she did not come in. She told me she found someone else to see her because I could not see her quickly enough. I did not handle what came next very well. I made many mistakes. I got confrontational and spoke to her in the heat of my emotions. I called her entitled; she called me nasty. Sometimes it is just too easy and gratifying to hit that send button.

I realized another lesson: repetition and practice are a huge part of spiritual and emotional growth. It is never one and done. The very thing I was writing about, I was messing up. I did not let my emotions cool down and speak my truth kindly, I forgot that part. But I will try better next time. God will give me all the chances I need to get this right. The key to achieving the best boundary repair with the least collateral damage is to wait and let myself calm down. This allows the issue to crystallize in my mind then I can articulate myself clearly and kindly to the other person.

When I am in calm delivery mode, this gives the other person the best chance of understanding me and not getting defensive. This is an internal boundary that I must strengthen, to protect other people from **my** emotional overreactions. Terry Real gives a perfect analogy for this. In his book, *The New Rules of Marriage,* he describes A 2-layered boundary system.

Like an orange. The outer orange skin protects you from other people taking advantage of you. While the inner white skin is the internal boundary that protects other people from my volatility.

Knowing our needs and setting boundaries to protect them cuts a neat trail to navigate the thicket of life. No one should trample your soul and you should not trample theirs. Emotions come to alert you of a trespasser. But then the key is to *PAUSE* and give those messenger emotions a chance to cool down, then enlist your higher, calmer set of repair emotions to restore the boundary. The *PAUSE* lets you switch emotional gears. The intense emotions that came to alert you of the boundary breach cannot be the same emotions you use to repair it. That will never work out well.

On the flip side, if a person approaches you in anger, because they are sloppily attempting to repair a boundary, the key is to recognize what is happening and use that same *PAUSE*. To catch yourself in the act of getting riled up, insulted, or defensive. And stop. And listen. If someone is coming at us with anger, pause and listen for the need underneath the anger that is trying to express itself.

Be the bigger person and listen curiously and keenly for the need, the boundary that *we* have violated in *their* life to make their anger flare at us. When we do not reciprocate anger for anger, the situation will not escalate and the damage can be fixed. A person will calm down pretty quickly when their need has been heard and respected. And their love for you will come back stronger.

The Pause is the critical element for success in both scenarios, for creating your own boundaries and for heeding other people's boundaries.

The whole game of character growth boils down to **THE PAUSE**. Remember, inside the heat of the moment, to stop, take a breath, and reach for The Pause Button. *Inside The Pause is where hard-core spiritual growth happens.* Calm down and use the aggravations of daily life to practice reaching for The Pause. Aggravations are not a distraction to spiritual growth; they are the medium for it. I once heard something reassuring about Heaven; *If you go 7 days without aggravation you may have died and gone to heaven. Because in heaven, there is no aggravation.* Aggravation disappears up there. Why? because we no longer need the constant poking and prodding towards the evolution of our soul – that is the work for down here.

I am pretty sure, when we get back there, no one will annoy us. Doesn't that sound like heaven?

DISEASE

"There are those in medicine who believe that emotions play a role in all aspects of health and illness. I am one of them."— Dr. John Sarno

Our bodies are smart. Inside us lives every substance, chemical and compound necessary to heal ourselves. There is one vehicle that causes *accelerated* healing of the body, mind and soul – that vehicle is thought. Our body waits for direction from one command center, our mind.

Each organ and each cell knows how to repair itself. The moment we get sick, our bodies automatically get to work in the direction of healing. Think of the last papercut you had, it healed easily, all by itself. You had nothing to do with it.

What is the biggest boost we can give our body during healing? The emotional support of the heart and mind. The good thoughts and the good feelings. Refuat HaGuf (body health) trails like a loyal puppy on the heels of Refuat Hanefesh (spirit health).

Body and Spirit heal in tandem, with spirit leading the way. The innate intelligence of our body can be guided and amplified by our conscious thoughts. Dr. Bruce Lipton, a brilliant researcher in epigenetics, says we can actually turn our cells on and off with our thoughts. The receptors on the outer membrane of the cell are listening for direction. This is the science of Epigenetics.

"My body always goes towards healing"
"I will **not** inherit any disease that my parents have"
"My body gets healthier and stronger everyday"
"My hair gets thicker"
"My skin gets more radiant"
"I get sexier everyday"

These positive thoughts broadcast to the body powerful signals from our Command Center. Our cells are constantly scanning for transmission.

The indisputable proof that our thoughts affect our body is the sexual response. Look at the cascade of physical responses that happen all by themselves when we think sexy thoughts. If those erotic thoughts can easily elicit a strong sexual response, why can't healing thoughts produce a strong healing response? Our bodies react powerfully to our thoughts. Our thoughts are like long fingers extending from our minds, flipping switches on the outer membrane of our cells on and off.

Thoughts are real. They show up on our face. When my husband began replacing all the negative thoughts in his head with positive ones, a woman at our Shabbat table literally asked him if he got a face lift. I am not even kidding. That is how real this gets.

The beautiful energy created inside your head from your beautiful thoughts will shine out of your face and upgrade your whole body. Good thoughts are light from your eyes. Good thoughts are the cheapest anti-aging cream on the market. My husband's face looks smooth and wrinkle free.

When my husband had crippling back pain, a friend recommended Dr. John Sarno's book, *Healing Back Pain*. Dr. Sarno formally introduced me to the relationship between negative emotions and the physical symptoms they produce. He said, "To leave the emotional dimension out of the study of health and illness is poor medicine and poor science."

Once, during a therapy session, my spiritual therapist Stephanie was coughing and sneezing. She said out loud to herself, "I wonder why I am

> *Thoughts are real*

manifesting this cold?" I had no clue what she was talking about. Ten years later, I understand exactly what she was saying. It is simple: *each and every illness or symptom has an emotional component hiding underneath it.* Once we get exquisitely honest within ourselves about the possibility of that connection, we can heal.

Dr. Sarno says simply entertaining the notion that there may be an emotional component to your pain is enough to begin to heal. He saw people healing their back pain with the simple act of *acknowledging*, not even fixing, the repressed anger sponsoring it. On the emotional spectrum, the stronger the emotion we are suppressing, compounded by the length of time we have been suppressing it, the more severe the illness that can be produced. Suppressing feelings of fatigue and overwhelm for a month can produce a bad cough or flu. Suppressing powerlessness or rage for two decades can produce a stroke and heart attack. (Esther Hicks)

With pain and disease, the soul is jumping up and down to get our attention. The Persian Poet Rumi said, "These pains you feel are your messengers, listen to them."

Your *soul knows* that chronic physical pain is masking chronic emotional pain. It is your *mind* that needs to make that connection. This is a huge benchmark of the Waking Up process – realizing that chronic pain is a red flag waved around by your soul, desperately trying to get your attention. Once the physical pain arrives, your soul is hoping that your mind makes the connection and that you will begin to scan for the underlying emotional pain begging for release and relief. This is the work of life. To ask the physical pain what emotional pain it wants you to feel, and then listen for the answer.

My left hand has been slightly numb and tingly for a few years. I asked this chronic symptom what it wants from me. I heard the answer in my heart. It said, 'chill, slow down, trust God with all the details and enjoy more.' So, I work on that prescription.

I was recently in a rush to get to a gathering. It was dark outside, and, in my haste, I miscalculated my jump off a ledge at the Washington Monument and tore something in my left ankle. I rolled around in the grass like a downed horse. My ankle swelled up like a balloon. After the intense pain subsided, I heard my body say, *walk on it*. So, I held Josh's arm and we hobbled back to the hotel. All I could do, after we got back to our room, was lovingly caress my swollen ankle as I elevated it on the bed. As I rubbed it, I thanked it for creating for itself a neat little boot. I knew my body would produce every necessary nutrient inside that bubble of interstitial fluid to make the perfect repair. Then I asked my soul, why did this happen? The message I heard back was... "*slow down, you don't need to run everywhere. You will experience whatever you are supposed to. Also, this experience will help you remember how to bring healing to other parts of your own body and the bodies of others, by tapping back into these intense and reverent emotions of love and gratitude for the absolute brilliance your body demonstrated here.*"

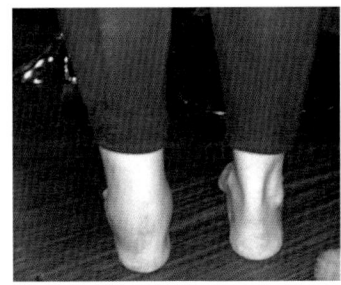

Swollen ankle

People misconstrue and reject the mind-body connection for two reasons:

1. They think it means that their physical pain is fake
2. They think it means that their disease is their fault

The opposite is true for both. The pain of the body is very real AND there is never reason to blame anyone, especially yourself, ever. Blame is wasted mental energy.

All this concept is asserting is that whatever illness you are experiencing, you have more influence over it than you think. You are not helpless to it. *You can be a proactive partner in your own healing in two ways:*

- Thinking good thoughts and feeling good feelings (to heal the soul)

- Good rest and healthy food (to nourish the body).

Take inventory of your emotions and figure out their connection to the pain. Only you can do this. No doctor can figure this out for you. Improve your self-care and self-acceptance. Love yourself a little more every day. Approach your own health from both directions, body and soul. And when you start to feel better, give yourself credit for doing the work. Do not dismiss your part in the healing; it is a huge spiritual accomplishment.

How can you start this process? You must dig deep and ask yourself, "Do I *really* want to get better?" I mean, do I really want my life to change that much?

Sometimes people don't. After a long time with a disease, it becomes a loyal companion, an identity, even a cause. People come to rely on all the perks their disease gives them—meaning, purpose, activity, sympathy, attention, nurturing, community, care, a break from life.

But, if you *sincerely* want to restore your own health, start by asking yourself some hard questions:

- What or who am I avoiding or trying to escape in my life?
- Am I overwhelmed?
- What sadness or anger am I not allowing myself to feel?
- What self-care needs have I been denying myself?
- Am I unhappy in my marriage, in my work?
- Do I need more downtime, more sleep?
- Do I want to retire?
- Do I feel sad that I never had any kids?
- Did my parents not give me enough attention, soothing, or security as a child?
- Is having this disease or numbing out with drugs and alcohol preferable to feeling the real issue going on in my life?

You can begin to heal if you answer these questions to yourself (no one else needs to know) with exquisite honesty and humility. You do not need to do anything more than acknowledge the connection to begin healing your disease.

At 21-years-old, a few months before my wedding, with no prior history, I developed asthma. I could not breathe at night, sleeping alone in my studio apartment on Broad

Street in Elizabeth, NJ as I worried about every detail of my future. I could not get enough air into my lungs. Doctors at the free clinic in my dental school listened to my symptoms and prescribed me an inhaler. Not a single person in my life thought to ask me about my emotional well-being when I told them my symptoms. I, myself, had no idea to connect my fears of getting married and starting dental school to my tight lungs. In hindsight, it was ridiculously obvious.

How can we rid every kind of disease from our body? By nullifying every kind of fear from our hearts.

Easier said than done.

Which is probably why the most repeated refrain inside the Bible is:

Do Not Fear

Fear is the wide tree trunk that all other negative emotions branch out from. These negative emotions, all rooted in fear, carry the potential to make us sick.

As we shrink the fear, we shrink the disease. But how do you shrink the fear?

Name it. Unmask it. Uncover it. Unearth it. Dig it out of your intestines.

Talk to the thing that scares you. Plop it on the table in front of you. Analyze it from all sides.

> *Fear is the wide tree trunk that all other negative emotions branch out from*

Be curious about it.

Take it outside for a walk. Try to understand it better. Laugh at it.

Make peace with it.

You will no longer need your body to divert your attention away from the fear, because you became friends with it. Getting playful with your fear diminishes its intensity. Then, after you shrink the fear really small, swap it out with trust.

Allow yourself to sink into the horrible feeling you have been avoiding. The tragic death, the guilt, the shame, the failure, the heartbreak, the rejection, the loneliness, the fear of abandonment, of being unlovable.

The horrible feeling will not stay forever. But let it stay as long as it needs to. Once you have honored the emotion by sitting with it, it will no longer need to get your attention through sickness later on.

Another trick is to share your grief with God. He promises to keep you company inside it. *Imo Anochi Batzarah (Psalms 101:15). I am with you in pain.* After you have felt the pain long enough and deep enough, He will help lift it from you. And the two of you will be tighter for having endured it together. You and God will emerge as partners in your recovery.

If you do get sick, there are two vital assessment questions to ask your heart:

1. What is my REAL pain?

In other words, what emotional turmoil is this disease coming to show me. Make the connection. Be real with it: name it, acknowledge it, feel what comes up and sit with it.

Am I lonely?
Am I afraid I will fail?
Am I afraid no one will love me?
Am I burying pain from my childhood?

Then, comfort the pain that rises up with soothing words from your soul. Let your soul offer nurturing comfort. Talk to your body, whisper the words of reassurance like you would lovingly offer a worried child. Stroke the cheek of your own face.

2. What unmet need has this disease come to show me?

Meaning, how does this disease serve me? This is called *secondary gain* in psychology. The disease is giving me a great excuse to avoid something else I do not want to face. This step is really hard to do. It takes great honesty and great humility.

Does this medical treatment give my empty days purpose and structure? Does this endometriosis help me feel more nurtured and cared for?

Does this fibromyalgia help me get the attention I have always craved? Does this vertigo give me a reason to rest and care for myself?

Does the herniated disk get me out of an overbearing financial responsibility? Does this depression or OCD behavior mask the sexual abuse I never faced?

Once you identify the unmet need or trauma the disease has come to show you, you can find healthier and more direct ways to address that need. Therapy, meditation, connection, yoga, any avenue of self-soothing. The disease did its job, it got you to the right place, and can now feel free to take leave of you.

We are all mostly just overgrown kids who did not get enough soothing and nurturing when we needed it the most. Give it to yourself now! Fill in those empty nurturing gaps. Stroke your own arm.

Let the lightbulb go off about illness. Even if you feel stupid at first. Make the connection.

I got this cold —maybe I needed a few days of rest because I feel overwhelmed at work.

I developed this type of cancer —maybe I needed more love and support from my family, or to be part of a community.

I have this autoimmune disease —maybe I needed something to give my days purpose and doctor appointments to fill my schedule.

I developed this addiction —maybe it helps me numb the pain of shame buried inside from my uncle who molested me.

These are exquisitely honest realizations to come to. I have done this work of digging deep inside. This is what I found. Disease comes to my body to help me acknowledge two specific things. One from my childhood and one from my current life.

Growing up in a busy house of eight children, I developed a baseline deficit of attention and connection. This need for more attention and connection still lurks inside me. I acknowledge it and try to find healthier ways to fulfill it, because I hate getting sick.

When I was about 10 years old, I remember faking terrible headaches to my mother. The worried, stricken look on her face made me feel so good inside, so cared for. My mother took me for testing. I remember having electrodes taped to my head to see if I had a brain tumor. It felt glorious, those moments of combined attention and focus from my mother and the doctors. That room full of concentrated concern was a heady rush to my neglected inner being. I thank God that I woke up and figured this out before I repeated this unconscious type of attention-seeking in my adult life. God really protected me with this one.

The other unmet need that lurks inside me in my current life is time to myself and rest. Simple as that. I work really hard at the office. My week is so busy. In order not to get sick, I take my weekends to do absolutely nothing. To just sit in my home and be. Guilt-free.

I want to tell you a different lesson about when I lost feeling in both my legs. It started on Rosh Hashana with a slight tingle in my feet, and by Succos, two weeks later, I was totally numb from the waist down. It was terrifying. I did not tell anyone except my husband. My instinct was *not to go to the doctor.* I thankfully listened to this primal wisdom from my gut. I knew somehow that if I heard a doctor, in a white coat, issue me a diagnosis, I would believe it. I wanted to protect my ears from the weighted words carried by a person of authority. I wanted to be my own authority. So, my husband and I went to Israel to speak to some very holy Rabbis instead. The Holy Rabbi Scheinberger of Jerusalem did not ask me one thing about the symptoms I presented to him.

Instead, he sent my husband out of the room. He took my hand, read my palm, and asked me if I was having problems with peace in my marriage. He knew the secret I would later learn from Louise Hay: when you heal your life, you heal your body. Disease always comes looking to help us heal something painful from the past or the present. Are you *willing* to look? That is the only thing you need to know.

Once I connected my physical symptoms to my emotional pain, they started going away. It took many months, but eventually I had a full recovery from whatever that numbness was. The most important thing I learned was not to be afraid of my physical symptoms. To instead use them as the impetus to look inside. Symptoms help me get curious; they keep me exploring and acknowledging the different unresolved emotions that need my attention. That is all they want. Symptoms are like little kids acting out. They settle back down when you give your inner emotional life more attention, more comfort, and more love.

Chronic diseases, more so than acute ones, are the body's cry to release a trapped emotion. An emotion suffocating under the surface. Let the physical pain bring forth the difficult memories and unwrap them carefully. You will know you are doing the work when recalling the same painful memory evokes less of an emotional charge. How can you measure that you made progress? When thinking about your past trauma does not hurt as much as it used to.

You feel a smaller lump in your throat. Your heart does not race as fast.

How can we prevent an emotion from getting trapped or stuck inside the body?

Feel the emotion in real time, as it comes up, and talk about it. Articulate it with a name. A simple conversation about it with yourself, another person, or even with God. Give yourself that perfect verbal outlet for a negative emotion to be released. Trapped emotions find their sweet release out the mouth.

What is the best *preventive medicine??*

Maintaining a *reservoir of joy* inside your heart that you can constantly dip into. Joy gives you vitality. Joy makes you magnetic to other people. Joy is your life force energy. The twinkle in your eye. This concept of Joy as Medicine dates back 200 years to the Vilna Goan, a famous Rabbi who lived in the 1700's.

He said, "A person who has mastered being in a joyous state will be able to cure himself of disease. Even though he might become ill, his Joy will heal him."

Getting sick is not a failure or a character flaw, it is an opportunity. Look for something inside your heart that needs acknowledging or something inside your life that needs changing. Disease is the call to get really clear on what is right or wrong in your life. To strengthen your voice, speak your mind, and get exquisitely honest with yourself and others.

When I get sick, I also do something else.

I remember, inside my heart, the different ages that my body healed itself from some pretty bizarre things. This gives the cells of my body a powerful shot of confidence. It reminds them that I trust them, historically, to know what they are doing.

Bell's palsy, age 10
Shoulder bursitis, age 19
Numb legs, age 29
Chronic hip pain, age 40
Frozen trigger thumb, age 42
Sprained ankle, age 45

All of these chronic diseases my body once manifested are now gone without a trace, thank you to God. Pretty wild. At the time, I thought they would never go away. Now, as I look back on each one, I am *experientially* reassured that my body knows exactly how to restore itself to full health. So does yours.

Chapter Fourteen

Forgiveness

In an interview on Super Soul Sunday, I heard Mitch Albom share something with Oprah. A priceless pearl that he picked up from Morrie:

"Forgive everyone, everything."

Those three little words sat me upright on my couch. It just does not get any simpler than that.

I felt this unmistakable *airport feeling* come over me. The weightless feeling, I get the moment I turn and walk away from the check-in counter. The instant freedom that descends immediately after handing over all my baggage. So light, I could skip through the airport. That is what forgiveness can do. There are two thoughts that can absolve anyone (including yourself) of any past wrongdoing. One is practical. One is spiritual.

Practical: They (I) did not know better. If they (I) knew better, they (I) would have done better. (Maya Angelou) They (I) were not at a level of self-awareness to have acted any differently.

Spiritual: Whoever wronged me was merely acting an agent of God sent to carry out His Will. Because there is *Nothing Besides Him*. I can forgive the mortal messenger easily. The entire event was ordained from Above or it would never have happened. Believing this in your bones will bring true forgiveness to any situation. Everyone is a cosmic pawn on God's 3-D chess board.

Always get yourself out of harm's way and remove yourself from chronic abuse situations. Do not stay somewhere that requires forgiveness every single minute. But to carry anger, resentment, bitterness, or grudges from the past, inside your heart for the long-term, is like your soul lugging heavy luggage all around the airport with no wheels. Check that load curbside and walk away.

Forgive everyone everything, including yourself. If I wronged someone or hurt someone or acted stupidly, either I did not know better at the time, or for some reason God used me to carry out His Will. Which is why I pray, as often as I can, hands to heaven, that Heaven please use me to carry out only good.

The Five-Second Forgiveness Formula:

> Seek forgiveness from others. Seek forgiveness from yourself. Grant forgiveness to others. Grant forgiveness to yourself.

God renews Creation every single day and in doing so shows us mortals how to do it. How to let yesterday go and let today be brand new. Hold nothing heavy from the past. Drop it. Be happy. Be light. Let the sun come up fresh.

> "View each day as the first day of your life. Have a fresh view of things each and every day."
> —Rabbi Yeruchum Levovitz.

TESHUVA

Teshuvah means *to return.* Teshuva is a different process than forgiveness.

Forgiveness helps humans drop the baggage of the past, Teshuva is the process to re-establish Intimacy with God.

God is constantly available to clean our slate.

Why? So, there is no old baggage sitting on the conveyor belt, getting in the way of our return to Intimacy with Him.

The memory on God's hard drive has a three-step instruction on how to permanently delete an error. The control/alt/delete combination that prompts a fresh connection to the Universe.

The three steps of Teshuva are easy to remember. They encompass all three phases of time: past, present, and future. They are:

PRESENT: Confess what you have done

PAST: Regret what you have done

FUTURE: Take it upon yourself to never do it again

This simple (not easy) formula is the trifecta God gave us to permanently delete our wrongdoings from His Memory and come back to Him brand new. It is a factory reset. (Wrongdoings that involve other people sometimes require asking their forgiveness as well.)

> *Forgiveness helps humans drop the baggage of the past*

There is no statute of limitations or expiration date on the Teshuva process. You will never be locked out for exceeding the number of attempts. You can return to God every hour, every minute, every day. God will never stop loving us, accepting us, or forgiving us. His arms are extended in a permanent outstretched position.

I watched an interview on YouTube with an Israeli teenager who experienced an NDE in 2015. He experienced 15 minutes of clinical death. The only snippet I remember is the part he recalled about Teshuva. This boy said he was shown all his sins, except the ones he did Teshuva for.

They were gone, totally deleted. Teshuva can also have a tremendous impact on human relationships. We can apply this three-step process of return not only to God, but to each other.

We all know how horrible it feels when someone you thought had forgiven you brings your sin up again. Teshuva is the remedy for this. True teshuva with people and with God obliterates all memory of the sin, like it never happened. The relationship has a chance at a fresh reboot after the Confession-Remorse-Promise combination has been activated. "I did it, I'm sorry, I won't do it again." Now, we can embrace each other with a fresh feeling. Guilt and shame have been wiped off that plate. So clean, you can see your own reflection again.

Each step of Teshuva reaches inside the Ego to diminish it. Each part of the Confession-Regret-Promise process unmasks another layer of the Ego and returns us to the arms of Humility. Teshuva releases the trapped corners of the soul pinned down by the heel of the Ego and releases you back up to God, light as a feather.

Step One: Confession

Confession is ground zero. Admit the mistake to yourself, to God, and to whoever else needs to hear it. The admission of sin begins the process of our soul humbly stepping forward. Take that pause to notice and subdue the powerful presence of Ego that always wants to block this first step.

The ego, in an effort to protect itself, also tries to step forward with a strong urge to *rationalize* our wrongdoing or *be defensive* about it. Recognize these two lower responses as Ego. Let your soul step forward with a more humble response instead, a sincere confession. *Yes, I did do it.*

I once did something horrible, almost unforgivable, to my husband. He asked me to speak the words of what I did to him. He needed to hear my confession. That moment is crystallized in my memory. It was incredibly humbling; the whole world went silent. My confession was the beginning. It shifted the imbalance of ego in my soul and removed my Ego's armor. It was the start of our healing. Confession made my soul accessible again, to myself and to my husband.

The Ego resists confession. The ego thinks confession will bring the world crashing down. The ego thinks confession will weaken us. The ego wants to protect us from whatever shame, disgrace, or loss will come from this embarrassing confession.

If only the ego understood how powerfully attractive confession is. Confession is an act of supernatural might. It is sexy. Whenever I see other people do it, I am in awe of their raw strength. They are willing to take whatever consequences their confession will bring in order to experience a fresh reboot of their soul.

Confession is no small thing. Confession is the formal groundbreaking in the Teshuva process. Confession opens the door and invites the soul inside to take the next step.

Step Two: Regret

Sincere regret is a beautiful, private, and rare thing to behold. Inside a moment of regret, there is holiness. The Ego is silent while the humble soul steps timidly into unsure waters. It bravely exposes itself to the possibility of condemnation in the exquisite hope of being met instead with kindness. Regret is vulnerability in motion.

I posit that the Original Sin was not merely the instant that Eve took a bite of the forbidden apple. The greater sin was that Adam's first reflex, when approached by God, was to snap back at Him with Ego. "This woman you gave me, she made me do it." Zero remorse.

Adam used three of the Ego's favorite tactics of diversion, blaming, and defensiveness, effectively obliterating steps one and two of Teshuva: confession and regret.

> *Regret is vulnerability in motion*

This may have been the very first instance Ego reared its ugly head in the history of creation. There is nothing that slams down the gate of conversation quicker than defensiveness.

Defensiveness blunts communication — accountability opens it up.

Here is how to discern the difference: Accountability tends to pause and listen before answering, defensiveness lashes out a reflex answer. At the beginning of any confrontation, the choice looms overhead: do I answer quickly with ego or thoughtfully with soul? What stance will I take – open hearted or closed? Hardened or vulnerable? Adam lashed out a reflex answer to God with Ego. Maybe that was why he had to leave the Garden. In the moment of blaming Eve, Adam closed his heart to God and put up the first barrier in their relationship.

Kane did the same thing. God approached him with a soft opener, "Where is Able your Brother?" Kane answered with an even worse device, *cynical* defensiveness, "Am I my brother's keeper?" He slammed the door hard in God's face. Kane was eyeballs deep in rationalizing mode. Zero accountability. Zero remorse.

If we are to correct these primordial sins, we must let that first *whoosh,* as Terry Real named it, pass by and then respond with our wiser, more connected, more humble self. The more you do it, the better you get at it. Life will give you plenty of chances to practice. Trust me.

There is nothing sexier or more immediately endearing than someone who takes ownership and accountability for something that has gone wrong. It is the highest level of humility and self-confidence not to get defensive when approached with a criticism.

My husband Josh has been my teacher in this. He showed me how to perform this art of true accountability. When he first woke up, he began to understand the horror of his past ways and how they affected me. When memories of his silent treatment and controlling, jealous behaviors all came flooding back to him in a tidal wave, he was truly horrified at himself. He was haunted by the sudden and profound understanding. I remember a moment in our bedroom, seeing him slumped on the edge of his bed. He had tears running from the outer corners of his eyes and he said words I will never forget. "'Tell me everything I ever did to you. Any time you remember something, I want you to tell me right away. And I will just listen and apologize."

I remember the word *contrition* lit up like a neon sign in my mind. I had to google the exact definition later that night: *sorrow for and detestation of sin with true purpose of amendment*.

I think it was the first time in my 42-year life that someone showed me how this word looked in person. He was the sweet and humble embodiment of Contrition. He was sitting there, so sorrowful and so brave all at once. He imprinted in my mind's eye a concrete mental image of this elusive spiritual concept, one that I can always refer back to: *true human remorse*. He had it. I saw it.

Remorse is the singular thing parole boards and juries look for in deciding the fate of the convict sitting in front of them. Does the face of this criminal show true remorse? If yes, they will judge him with a kind eye and give him a second chance at life. Remorse revives our mutual feelings of humanity towards each other. It was the thing that saved my marriage. I was able to see my husband as a person again.

I reach back into that bedroom memory when I need a visual instruction for how to do remorse properly: with ownership and accountability. When I am approached with a criticism or anything that threatens my Ego, this is the moment for me to gather that inner vulnerability that says, "There isn't anything I have done that I can't come back from, simply by listening with curious empathy and apologizing sincerely for whatever I did to hurt this other human being." The Ego is the thing inside us that shows its fangs and gets defensive. Anytime you assign blame or get defensive, you can know **for sure** it is your Ego talking. The soul is hovering over the Ego and gently nudging it to lay down that sword and simply listen to what this other soul is trying to convey. The best chance of calming down any situation is to listen and apologize. This is a skill hard-earned by the soul.

My friend was struggling to forgive her husband for an issue they had in the past. She was beating herself up for not being able to forgive him and move on. I had a flash of insight and asked her,
"Well, is he showing you any remorse about it?" She said, no, not really. I understood from her experience that we can Forgive Everyone, Everything. However, we cannot fully accept them back into our hearts and lives until they give us this profound offering of true remorse.

> *Anytime you assign blame or get defensive, you can know for sure it is your Ego talking*

If God Himself needs remorse to erase the past, we need it, too. Remorse is the crucial hinge that returns us back to love. God even goes so far as to say that when we show remorse He will turn our sins into good deeds. I understood how God can switch that up after Josh showed me his remorse. After seeing his remorse, every hurtful thing Josh had done to me lost its negative emotional charge inside my memory. It all looked cute and adorable in hindsight because he felt so bad about it.

Every time we reach for the higher version of ourselves and let our soul step forward to take ownership of our mistakes (instead of rationalizing or becoming defensive) we make a small repair to the Original Injury of Adam and Kane's defensive responses to God.

I wonder sometimes how different the world might look had these original humans used this basic three-step process, "I messed up, I'm sorry, I will try never to do that again." How fortunate that we were given the basic instructions of Teshuva to be able to do better now.

In summary, Regret follows on the heels of Confession. Speak the sin and allow the ensuing awful feelings to flood your heart. Understand and internalize that you disappointed God, yourself, another person, or all three. Feel the regret deeply. Express it in all the ways your face and body know how. Like any emotion, feel it fully so it can bring you right up to the doorstep of Step 3.

STEP THREE: Accept upon yourself to never do it again.

Step three is crucial. It causes the powerful shift of restoring you back to your full emotional vigor and vitality. How? By giving *HOPE* towards a better future. This third step moves you out of the stagnant, murky energy-field of regret, into the vibrant energy-field of hope.

Regret is painful – you never want to get stuck in step two. The Hope of a better future has enough energetic force to pull us out from under the heavy drag of the past. Regret starts to abate when we can sit comfortably with an imperfect aspect of our past and commit internally to do better in the future. Every thought of Hope for the future swaps out thoughts of regret from the past.

This last step is the sweet spot of the Teshuva process. It is the part that awakens Hope inside yourself and the other. When the offending one tells the offended one, *I will do better next time*, both hearts perk up. The anticipation of changed behavior and a better future gives both parties sweet relief. The delivery of changed behavior brings a peaceful completion to this Teshuva process, and we can all move on.

Chapter Fifteen

Attention

A few years ago, I found myself in Albany, NY for a couple of days. My daughter's mock trial team made it to the state-level competition. It was a brief two-day stint outside my normal life. Unfamiliar surroundings always feel vivid and inviting to me. Whenever I find myself somewhere new, my eyes take in life with a more playful curiosity. I was enjoying dinner with my husband and daughter in a dimly lit, somewhat makeshift kosher vegan restaurant, after an intense day of watching her compete. On the way to use the bathroom, I noticed a peach-colored sign hanging right outside the bathroom entrance. It said, "Do All Things With Love." This bland, unassuming wall art caught my soul. I halted, gazed, pondered its meaning, and snapped a quick picture of it.

This sign made me wonder something I had never wondered before. HOW ON EARTH can I *Do All Things With Love*, I mean, practically speaking? I wanted an instruction manual.

I thought about it for a while and came up with three ways:

1. Manipulate and mold my thoughts until they generate an energy-field of Love around myself.

    - "This morning sky is so calming."

    - "My UPS guy has a pure soul from God."

    - "My husband is always trying so hard to make me laugh."

    If I conjure relaxed, easygoing, loving thoughts, they transport me inside a balmy, breezy atmosphere of Love. Palm trees everywhere. Any action I take from inside this invisible field automatically carries the current of Love inside it.

2. Slow down. Nothing loving was ever done in a rush. No connection was ever established with one eye on the clock. This is a big one for me. As a dentist on a schedule, I am always tethered to the clock – I never want to keep anyone waiting too long. "Life on the treadmill," is how my sister Leah describes this. She nailed it perfectly. Less rushing and more savoring is probably the most effective way I can Do All Things With Love. *I think the gaping regret I would have at the end of it all is that I didn't slow down and enjoy my life as much as I could have.* If I am darting around like a squirrel on crack, I am missing the lush and languid paradise all around me.

3. This brings me to the epiphany that surprised me most about Love. It turns out that *Love is the same thing as Attention*. These two words are

practically **interchangeable**. Whenever I give my full Attention to anything, I also end up Doing All Things With Love.

I understood this concept more deeply from the movie *Ladybird.* In one scene, Ladybird is sitting across from the head nun who is sitting behind her desk. They begin discussing her college essay. The conversation goes like this:

Nun: "I read your college essay, you clearly love Sacramento." Ladybird: "I do?"

Nun: "You write about Sacramento so affectionately and with such care." Ladybird: "I was just describing it."

Nun: "Well, it comes across as Love." Ladybird: "Sure, I guess I pay Attention."

Nun: "Don't you think maybe they are the same thing, Love and Attention?"

Pause.

Mind blown.

Maybe everyone else in the world already knew this. But in that moment, in that movie, I got it—for the first time. Love and attention are the same thing.

> *Whenever I give my full Attention to anything, I also end up Doing All Things With Love*

To sum up, there are 3 Steps for doing all things with love:

- Think loving thoughts
- Slow down
- Pay Attention

When your actions and words carry the Energy of Love inside them, they become powerful agents for change. Actions and words with love held inside them heal your heart, accelerate results, and make yourself and the people around you feel inexplicably happy. Your life becomes slick and productive when it is juiced up on love.

In the book, *The Art Of Hearing Heartbeats*, the main character, Mi Mi, rolled cigars with so much love and tenderness that everyone who bought them and smoked them fell in love. She made lots of money and changed the world for the better. Love brings with it abundance in all directions. Doing All Things With Love is a win- win for any creature held inside its perimeter. All types of love flourish inside the giving and receiving of Attention. A bond of love is created between any two creatures in the mutual paying attention of each other. A channel of warmth is opened up inside this private give and take. Souls connect through the warm flush of held eye contact. That extra two seconds of sustained, loving eye contact can save a life.

Love is the quiet, unhurried, undivided Attention you give the other. Love materializes wherever you rest the full weight of your steady, open-hearted gaze and when you

> *Love brings with it abundance in all directions*

open yourself to receive the gaze being offered by the other. The magic happens both ways.

When I remember to pause and do this exact thing with God inside prayer and meditation, I start to feel intense affection for Him. Throughout my day, in small moments, I slow down and *Pay Attention* to His presence. I rest my gaze on any aspect of His creation. The sky. The trees. The moon. My kids. My husband. The patient in my chair. This is how I nourish our relationship and share my life with Him. I start to feel Him inside everything, and He starts to feel very REAL.

What is the goal of life here on earth? To FEEL God as REAL through the practiced art of Paying Attention to all that He has created. Attention to any living thing is a form of Attention to God. This is because He is inside every animal, mineral and vegetable. When you give attention to any living thing, you are giving attention to God. God is also with us on the inside —through our sensations. Paying attention to every pleasurable sensation of the body is another form of paying attention to God. Every sip of hot coffee, bite of crunchy sandwich, warm hug, foot rub —all belong to Him. When we pay attention to the pleasures of life, we are paying attention to God.

When I told my daughter Kaila about my ladybird epiphany, she said the most stunning thing back to me. She said, "Of course, Mom. Remember what Elie Wiesel said: 'The opposite of Love isn't hate, it's indifference.'" Omg. Kaila's immediate understanding blew me away. The opposite of love is not *hating someone*, it's paying *no attention at all* to someone. Hate is still a form of attention.

Plants and the souls of small children wither and die inside the desolate wasteland of No Attention.

We all understand how deeply unsatisfying and stinging it feels to receive half of someone's attention. When someone looks down at their phone when you are mid- sentence or past you at a party. When the Doctor is in a rush and not really listening to you. It is so quietly shaming and diminishing.

There was an interaction with a patient that burned this lesson into my heart. I was running late and, in a rush, the entire morning. Probably for a million legitimate reasons I cannot remember. My first patient was in the chair, and I whirled into the treatment room barely saying hi to him. I turned to the computer and began blabbing about what we were going to do. He was just watching me. With an amused and playful tone he said, "You can slow down now."

I had to swallow an immediate lump in my throat. The kind way he said those five words did a million things to my heart in an instant: He reminded me that I was a person. He reminded me that he was a person. He reminded me to slow down. To pay attention to life. To connect. To care for myself. To care for him. To savor life. What good is accomplishing any goal or checking off any item on my to do list if I have not savored a single one? This patient, in the most caring and lighthearted way, reminded me of life's most important thing, to slow down and pay attention. I still need to work on this.

Hebrew language teaches us something profound. The Hebrew way to say Attention is a brief two-word instruction. A verb that constantly refreshes itself. The

Hebrew for Attention is actually a phrase, **Sim Lev** - meaning, **to place your heart upon.** What is the best way to pay Attention? To place your heart on something. Over and over. To be a Lover of the world is to be a Slow- Paced, Joyful, Attention-Giver. To become a noticer of small details. Why else would God have put those tiny black spots on the back of a ladybug?

LISTENING

The other suffers as long as he is in need of someone to listen to him. And you- you are the person who can do it. If someone has to have recourse to a psychotherapist, it is because no one in the house can listen… An hour spent in this way can already relieve a great deal of another person's pain. (Pg 37 *True Love*, Thich Nhat Hanh)

King David in the Psalms, eight different times says to God, *Bend your ear to me.* Not once does he say, *Turn your mouth to me.* When we seek comfort we seek Listening. A bent ear conjures an image of easy, familiar connection; of unburdening yourself to a trusted soulmate, of a whispered conversation between close confidantes. Our ear is the receptive instrument of our soul. When we listen with our soul, we heal the one talking. We invite them to sit inside the healing space of our soul and unload. **Presence** is simply our Soul that has floated to the surface and hovers there to witness, understand, and comfort. We do not have to say ONE WORD.

> *The Hebrew for Attention is actually a phrase, Sim Lev - meaning, to place your heart upon*

In fact, if you really think about it, the word *Presence* becomes interchangeable with the word Soul. When we engage any of our five senses inside the open state of Presence, we experience unity of body and soul. You can smell with Presence, taste with Presence, touch with Presence, see with Presence, hear with Presence. That just means you are calm and conscious as you use the tools of your body. You become tuned in as your soul filters in all the soothing tones of dusk. You start to share every sensual pleasure together with God.

This leads me to The Art of Holding Space. To listen with an open, curious heart is an expert tool of healing. To sit comfortably while another soul shares what is really going on below (Leonard Cohen). To resist the urge to give advice, to tell a story about yourself, to fix something, or be curious about things they do not want to share. To recognize the different voices of the Ego as they poke their heads up.

Anytime you listen calmly and neutrally, without getting offended-angry-triggered-defensive-curious, your *own soul is swelling and growing while the other soul is healing.* This is a character flaw my soul came back to have another shot at—to just Listen. When people start telling me a problem, my brain immediately wants to give advice, fix it, tell my own story or be nosy.

My Ego does this for a few reasons.

Sometimes I want them to think I am smart.

Sometimes their pain makes me feel annoyed or uncomfortable.

Sometimes I want to do a quick fix and rescue them.

Sometimes I think they should be farther along on their spiritual journey already! I am unconsciously taking the 'one up' position, as Terry Real named it. He defines 'One up' as grandiosity. Looking down at someone from this position of Ego will never create the environment for healing, which is truly the gift my soul wants to offer.

I once went to a marriage therapist and at the end of the session completely lost my mind, cursing and screaming. She triggered me bad. At the very end of the session, after I had just spilled half my heart, she turned to my husband and asked him a question so off-topic that I felt completely unheard with everything I had just opened up about during the session. It took me a day to figure out why I lost my mind. So I reached out to her by text the next morning to explain. When I told her that the perceived dismissal of me was what made me lose my mind, she would not get down from her professional high horse and apologize. She simply defended her position and told me I have more trauma work to do. Which is true. But I could never go back there. She would not go soul to soul with me and allow her vulnerability to come through and just hear me or apologize. I knew healing could never happen for me in an environment like that. Her soul was too unavailable.

This is why Terry Real's therapy works: he does not put himself in the 'One Up', all-knowing position that many therapists take. He stays level with the patient, eye to eye, soul to soul. No Bullshit. He bucks the rules of conventional therapy and I love him for it. He offers his patients real conversation with sincerity and transparency. He trains other therapists using a completely refreshing paradigm, "Say *to* the patient what you would say to other therapists *about* the patient at the water cooler."

Therapy that wields the combined energy of Listening and Honesty can work rapid miracles. It has flexibility, authenticity, and realness to it. That combination can slice through layers of bullshit and really move things. The healing we can accomplish in one hour with our therapist's full attention and frank truth-telling, is life altering.

I figured out another reason I do not just shut up and listen to people. I realized that I am uncomfortable with witnessing them in pain, so I divert by throwing unsolicited advice at them. I have to practice sitting comfortably with pain, other people's and my own, knowing that we all take turns inside hurt. If my real goal is to help them suffer less, listening with my soul is the most efficient way I can accomplish this.

Holding the candle, the presence of soul, to illuminate someone else's pain, is one of the greatest pain relievers we can give. King David is grateful for this. "Because You light my candle, Hashem, my God, You illuminate my darkness." (Psalms 18:29) When someone is in pain, they are raw; their soul is vulnerable and exposed. If we meet that soul with our soul, instead of our Ego, we bring companionship to that soul. Listening has the transformative power even the world's best advice could not touch. If I remember that my end goal is to help relieve the suffering of that person, I will close my mouth and bend my ear.

When we just listen and ask gentle questions, we trust the other soul to tap into its own wisdom. We have faith in that soul's ability to figure out all by itself what it needs. Listening confers a silent confidence to that soul that you trust it to bravely elevate itself out of the misery.

When a person feels fully heard, their pain can dissipate inside the open space your soul created for them and the lesson that soul needs can emerge without you having said one word.

I used to do this horrible thing as a young mother. I was stupid and operating in survival mode, totally unconscious. There were times I remember when one of my kids got hurt (gulp) and I would yell at them. My oldest daughter once fell off her bike and I ran over and yelled at her for not being more careful. I still feel like a monster when I think about it. I was trying to dispel my own discomfort and ended up putting more on her, instead of just being calm and present to her pain. It was awful of me. I hope she forgives me.

Now I try to go alongside someone who is in physical or emotional pain. To help them feel less alone while they are in pain. This is all I want when I am in pain: someone to keep me company until it passes. I try not to have the reactions that would feel yucky to me if I was in pain:

1. Over-Empathizing (your pain is making me uncomfortable, so I will hijack the emotion and make it about me)

2. Owning their problem (fix it mode, lack of boundaries)

3. Giving unsolicited advice (ego talking, I know better)

4. Becoming hysterical (create diversion, making it about me again)

5. Becoming too worried (not trusting their innate wisdom)

All of these diversional tactics prevent the soul from simply sitting still and Listening.

Buddhist monk Thich Nhat Hanh first introduced me to this concept of deep Compassionate Listening. I could feel this man's holy presence touch me through the TV screen.

He said, "To listen with only one purpose, to help him or her **empty her heart,** and if you remember that, you are helping him or her to suffer less." Full Listening can bring at least Half the Healing. Allowing someone to spill out the pent-up emotions inside their heart is like allowing a nauseous person to finally throw up. You feel so much better after.

When someone else is talking, they are giving you a glimpse into their perception of the world. The way they filter is different from the way you filter. If you have ever had the confusing experience of logging onto someone else's Facebook page thinking it was yours, you understand what it means to see the world through a starkly different perspective. No two feeds are the same.

When we honor someone else's perspective with the pure goal of trying to understand it, we have opened a space for them to heal whatever has wounded them. They feel heard, validated, and supported.

If we combine Compassionate Listening with a beautiful teaching from Wayne Dyer, **"See the light in others and treat them as if that is all you see,"** you will bring a powerful combination to people. A healing Presence that needs no credit, that has set Ego aside. Soul supporting soul. Compassionate listening tells the other person, we have different minds and bodies, but our souls, they are the same and I trust yours.

Chapter Sixteen

Kids

I remember being a kid.

I remember wanting adults to look at me, not through me or past me. I wanted them to meet my seeking eyes and engage me like the sentient being I knew I was. I wanted respect, warmth, and connection. I just did not know what to call these things at the time. I wanted them to notice the full-sized adult squeezed into the tiny body that I knew I was.

When I interact with kids now, I look at them with the full weight of my soul. I want them to know that I can see the sentient being inside them.

When you see a kid's soul, they will give you the best gift in return: prolonged eye contact that never gets weird.

Mary Tyler Moore had a son who committed suicide.

She said, "I wanted to be a perfect mother, I wanted to teach Richie the things I wasn't taught. It didn't occur to me then that the most important issue for my child was to learn, *by my Attention,* that he mattered."

To give your child loving, patient Attention is everything they crave. It is tantamount to seeing their soul. Kids need their soul to be seen or it dies a thousand painful deaths. They bury parts of their soul to protect it from further injury and the Ego steps in to protect it. The ego, the non-connected part of the personality, the part that only sees the self, becomes the soul's armor. When a child's ego grows within them, it does the saddest developmental damage. It blocks receptivity to connection and access to inner wisdom. It blocks the growth of humility and insight. It blocks the relationship to God and constricts the soul.

Children, whose souls are not nurtured, develop heartbreaking coping mechanisms. They act on the outside the chaos they are feeling on the inside. They harden their spirit. A hardened spirit can turn into a full-blown personality disorder as an adult. Personality disorders do not come out of nowhere. They happen when the soul went underground because connection was too painful or too unavailable to them as a child. Neglected or abused children become hardened versions of themselves. They never learn how to connect to themselves and to other people. It can take a lifetime or several lifetimes to recover the wounds inflicted in these early years.

Parenting expert Dr. Shefali Tsabary says, "When you are a parent, it's crucial you realize that you aren't raising a 'mini me' but a spirit throbbing with its own signature." This tiny soul mapped out its life plan with God long before it came out of your body. A holy plan, whose first stop on its long itinerary was your uterus. This is a distinguished honor. God and that soul both deemed your uterus a worthy entry point.

The four vital things you can provide this soul that chose you are — Love, Attention, Connection and Support. Then it is your job to step out of its way. Nourish innate talents and inclinations. Support enthusiastically ideas that naturally excite this soul. Sign them up for ballet or art or computer classes, once you notice that is what they are drawn to.

Never impose limits or beliefs of how we think their life should look. Most importantly, *never make your unlived dreams their invisible responsibility.* Never restrain their wildest dreams out of fear or even jealousy. We must hold this soul in awe and let it flourish wildly in the direction of its own destiny.

> *The four vital things you can provide this soul that chose you are — Love, Attention, Connection and Support*

"Be good company" to your children, advises Sadhguru.

Not an authoritarian know-it-all or a controlling task master.

Be their open-hearted, ever-available refuge from the storm of life.

According to biologist Dr. Bruce Lipton, we have from age 0-7 to program our children. These are the years children are open sponges. Children walk around in a dreamlike, hypnotic, theta brainwave state during these early years, similar to the hazy moments right before and after sleep where reality and imagination blend seamlessly. Theta brain waves give open access to the subconscious mind. Children's brains soak in and believe all they witness and hear. These years become their subconscious reference point. All of us flip back to our mental rolodex of beliefs we acquired as children, mostly without even knowing that it was written by our parents and caregivers, not by us. Our most crucial job as parents is to program their hard drive well, coded with immutable sequences of love, joy, and acceptance.

*Spark their tiny neural connections with **love**, not fear.*

This is the whole, entire secret of parenting. Say encouraging words to them as often as possible:

> The world will rise up to support your dreams. God loves you; I love you.
>
> Your body is beautiful, healthy, and smart.
>
> You will always have everything you need, easily.
>
> Good ideas will always come to you at just the right moment.
>
> Money will come to you easily, straight from God's treasure chest.
>
> You live in a world of plenty and abundance.

When this positive programming gets hard-wired as Truth into their subconscious, their world will automatically rise to meet these beliefs. Dr. Lipton says it can be no other way: "The function of the mind is to create coherence between our beliefs and the reality we experience." There is a magical congruence, an invisible cause and effect, between inner beliefs and outer reality.

This concept fuels *The Secret* and *The Matrix*. These books and movies are brilliant efforts to shake up and wake up our souls to remember that we are active and optimistic co-creators of our own lives. They motivate us to break the illusion of suffering and fleece the faulty programming of scarcity and competition we have received as kids.

There is one concept parents should grasp during these crucial early years. The one piece of advice I wish that I practiced more when my own kids were little: Engage with your child's soul and nourish it with love.

How can I accomplish this practically?

Easy.

With warm eye contact.
With steady, reliable, ever available

Attention. With safe arms to run to.

By establishing yourself as home-base for

dependable kindness.

Finally, by lifting your head when they talk

to you and waiting until they finish what

they have to say before you say a word.

Toni Morrison changed the entire game of raising healthy children with one question. "When your child enters the room, does your face light up?" If this is the only parenting change you ever make, it is enough. When we handle a child's soul with care, we are acknowledging something Holy: That God created them and delicately transferred them into our human hands to take it from there. Imagine how hard that must have been for God. Think about how excruciating it is to leave your kid with a babysitter you know is mostly clueless and incompetent. What a sacred trust God has extended to us.

What lifelong gift do we give our kids by seeing their soul? They will learn the most enduring skill, how to ethically-mine and locally-source their self-esteem from the only reliable place — from *inside* their soul. A child knows that they are foremost a soul. Our responsibility is to make sure they do not forget it. We want them to carry this authentic, soul confidence into adulthood.

If a child's self-esteem is hung up on anything outside themselves, like beauty, brains or accomplishment, it is very precarious. It can be lost. Seeing your child's soul every day will tether it tight to their inner consciousness. They will grow to be authentic, humble, confident and ever connected to their vast inner space. They will discover that their Inner Space is as vast and galactic as Outer Space.

They will create their life from that wondrous Quantum field. This is the greatest gift. This is the best way to ensure their success in life. When their looks, brains, or abilities fall short or disappoint them, the connection to their own soul and all its goodness never will. They will know their own divine worth. They will understand in their bones that they belong to Eternity. They will worry less. They will forever be able to geo-locate and connect to their soul inside, and to the Creator Himself, because your loving eye contact showed them how.

Whenever I feel intimidated about speaking publicly or interacting with a really good looking or brilliant person, I say four words inside my head. Four words that Oprah taught me. "Lead with your soul," she said. These powerful words harness and re-direct my soul to shine through the lens of my physical eyes. My radiant soul brings to the surface much more confidence than my fragile ego does. When my normal eye contact starts to feel shy and self- conscious, the eye contact of my soul swoops in to bolster it and hold it steady. Try it sometime, it really works.

Four practical discoveries I have about parenting:

1. If a child approaches you with a brave confession or any type of truth-baring moment, immediately hug them, praise them, or dance with them. The *last* thing to do is embarrass or punish them. Whatever the offense — they stole a candy bar, bullied another kid, or ate dirt. If they are coming to you and telling you...they trust you! They came looking for you to help make it right. You temporarily hold the fragile privilege of being their safe place! This is a delicate honor. Do not blow it with the classical parental misstep of thinking it is your duty to punish them. If you punish them, you have slammed the door on them ever coming to you again. The safe place they hoped for, IN YOU, is now gone. Instead of playing the part of the adult, play the part of the friend. Look them right in the eye and say, "Thank you for trusting me! How can I help you make this right?" This will forge a synaptic connection for them — that telling the truth opens into a world of loving and playful acceptance. Condemn them and you risk them becoming liars for life. If you teach them that telling the truth whips up a shit storm, why would they ever risk that again? They opened a raw and vulnerable wound to you, and you threw salt in it. Be careful, their amorphous character gets shaped by your hands. Be present to your own soul, not worried about public opinion or what you "should" be doing as a parent. That is the best way not to mess these golden opportunities up.

   When I have a young kid in my dental chair, I lean in and ask them if they brush their teeth. Some kids astound me. They look right at me and say, no, they do not. I give them a wide-eyed look of love and surprise and immediately thank them for telling me the truth. I tell them it is more important to tell me the truth than it is to brush their teeth! Then, after I see that they have registered my glowing approval, I gently encourage them to do better with the brushing.

I have messed this and so many other things up as a mom, but the next discovery I am about to tell you about is pure gold. It is a universal remedy for any parenting fail. And when done right, can fix almost anything.

2. Sincerely apologize to your kid whenever it hits you that you messed up — **but** do not use the word **BUT**. The word *but* always goes back and erases whatever came before it. Replace *but* with **AND**. *But* immediately launches you into **defense** mode. **But** spews out some lame-ass excuse for why we did something wrong. The word *and*, on the other hand, launches you into **ownership** mode. *And* shows remorse and explains how you will make it right and try harder in the future, without the lame-ass excuse.

"I'm sorry I just snapped at you. That was wrong of me. It wasn't your fault, it was mine. I was tired, it was wrong of me *and* I will try my very best not to do that to you anymore."

This apology is light-years better than,

"I'm sorry I snapped at you *but* you were driving me crazy with all that noise you were making while I was trying to sleep." (that just put the blame back on the kid and is a fake-ass apology).

When you apologize right, kids feel like worthy human beings. They see a living model of what humility looks like.

They will see you as a human being trying your best and love you for it. Most importantly, they will learn from you how to apologize properly, with finesse, which will make them a really good spouse one day. We all know many adults who have no idea how to apologize (it might have been me). Perhaps they never witnessed an adult take ownership of a mistake when they were a child.

I was awful at apologizing. Josh taught me how. An apology done right is one of the best cultivators of Humility within the soul. A sincere apology sets the Ego aside while the soul steps out as the leader. Come to think of it...our egos are mostly comprised of the interpersonal skills we mislearned as kids. This early mislearning become the character work of our adult life.

3. I learned this next parenthood discovery from my Bubby. **Talk to God** out loud like He is in the room with you, in front of your kids. Have no shame about it. I saw my Bubby doing this when I was in the young ages of theta-hypnosis brain waves, 0-7 years old. I witnessed a Real Relationship through her and understood it in my soul.

At the end of this life, there is not one lasting inheritance you can leave to your kids. Money, homes, cars, even you, can all vaporize. There is only **one** thing you can give them that will literally last forever: A relationship with God.

How can you give them this?

Simple.

Talk to God in front of them like He is in the room. Because He is.

Once in a while, I will experience a rare phenomenon which I call, "A Perfect Moment." A Perfect Moment happens when a sense of heightened awareness, divine calm, and a slowing down of time all wash over me simultaneously. This fleeting sensation is a suspended, shimmering, slow- motion moment. I smile and enjoy this brief visit from the Angel of Peace. Like there is nothing else I need and nowhere else to be.

I remember one of these moments. I was taking my kids to see the movie "Thor Ragnarok." It was a cold, snowy, winter night and I parked my car near the theatre. We were nestled in our seats, quietly chewing the hot pizza that we had picked up on the way. We were warm, fed, and huddled together inside my steamy minivan. I felt the Perfect Moment feeling tingle up my left arm. I said, out loud, between bites, "Thank You Hashem for this Perfect Moment." Saying it out loud seals in the goodness.

The fleeting sensation of perfection becomes even more Transcendent when it is shared out loud with God. I try to teach my kids that, in a world made mostly of chaos, when a Perfect Moment hits, feel it, acknowledge it, and share it with God.

Perfect moment

Inside that shared moment of exquisiteness, God begins to feel Really Real

4. This next piece of advice is huge.

Be **Flirty Friends** with your spouse. Be playful and spontaneous with each other. Be kind and laugh easily.

When your kid feels an air of friendship in the house, all is right in their world. I remember the times my father or mother would laugh hysterically with each other. I would revel in that moment, my tiny soul exalted by their laughter. I also have the shimmering memory of my father grabbing my mother and dancing her around the kitchen. When parents are playful friends, a child's inner sense of well-being goes off the charts.

My next four parenting discoveries conveniently form a great acronym: **GATE.**

G: GOOD MOOD

People do not talk about moods enough. Moods are HUGE. It took me decades to figure out that when spiritual teachers speak about elevating your vibration, all they are talking about is your mood. Mood is such a tangible word for me to grasp.

Your good mood is a gift you give everyone inside your energy's reach. Your good mood creates the aura inside your energy field. If someone near you is in a bad mood, you always know it.

And if you are like me, you run.

When my husband woke up spiritually, the single thing I can point to as having changed was his mood. Moods are big, they affect life more than we give them credit for. Moods combine and add up to a personality. Moods are at the center of the Law of Attraction. You cannot attract anything good into your life from inside a bad mood.

There is nothing worse for a kid than a parent in a bad mood. Your mood is the invisible thing that fills up the whole house. Do whatever you need to get your mood right. Deep breaths. Meditate. Scream into a pillow. Listen to Esther Hicks videos.

If you cannot change your mood, explain to your children why you are in a bad mood and apologize. So they know it is not their fault. So it is less confusing for them. In a harsh environment with no explanation from you, kids will automatically blame themselves for your bad mood before ever blaming you.

My mother has always given us the gift of her constant and steady good mood. Whenever you call her, you know exactly who will pick up the phone. *Same Ima every time.* Her indestructible good mood gives me an invisible anchor in a tumultuous world. My office manager, Rifky, is the same. When she walks through the door every single morning, she brings the sunshine with her.

A: ATTENTION

Attention is the clearest and most understood form of love with kids.

Pay full attention to your kids when they talk, especially those first few minutes when they walk through the door. They will not repeat themselves if you have been spacing out. I have learned this the hard way.

T: TONE OF VOICE

"90% of friction in daily life is caused by wrong tone of voice."—author unknown

The content of our words is carried on the frequency of our tone. Tone of voice is our musical instrument to suffuse energy into our words. We can hear a muffled conversation and immediately understand in our primal gut if it sounds happy or stressed, annoyed or loving.

If we recorded ourselves, we would often be horrified by our tone of voice. It is a blind spot for most of us. Too harsh, too cynical, too hurried, too mean. When it comes to words, warm them up and slow them down. Filter your words through your heart valves. Regulate them like it is a game you are playing with yourself to generate as much love and encouragement and connection as you can. It becomes fun to see the effect that tweaking your tone of voice can have on those around you.

Whatever you say to your kids, it is your *tone*, not your words, that will tell them they are your biggest pleasure in life.

"At the end of the day people won't remember what you said or did, they will remember how you made them feel."-Maya Angelou.

Your tone of voice accomplishes what Maya is talking about. It is your tone that makes people feel things. Your facial expressions come in as reinforcements.

When my 17-year-old daughter asks me if three of her friends can have a ride home from high school, a "Sure, no problem," said in a tone of love, reassures and settles her nervous teenage heart. A resentful, annoyed tone wreaks invisible havoc on her fragile, forming psyche. And even worse, it can become her own learned, default tone. Kids are like parakeets; they blindly mimic tone. Sarcastic parents spawn sarcastic kids; mean parents create bullies. Your loving tone of voice secures you a legacy of kindness.

E: EXAMPLE

No amount of lecturing, instructing, insisting, or educating can accomplish what your **good example** effortlessly does.

Whatever it is that you wish your kids would do, all you have to do is *do it.*

When they see you doing it, they do it. Period. They are always watching.

The endgame, the ultimate reward of all this parenting effort, is the sweet feeling of something Jews call *NACHAS*. Nachas is a Hebrew word with no exact English translation. Nachas is like spiritual dividends.

I can only describe how Nachas feels to me. After having done my best and trusted God for the rest, there is no greater pleasure than sitting back and watching my kids make their way in this world. The heightened satisfaction of seeing my kids, who are spiritually and cellularly embedded in my heart and soul, bravely move towards their destiny, and to witness in awe, how the Universe rises up to support them all along the way – that is Nachas.

God trusted you to raise them, then you must release them back into the wild, knowing God will always find a way to catch them.

Chapter Seventeen

Dreams of the Heart

> *"We see with the eyes, but we see with the brain as well, and seeing with the brain is often called imagination."*— Oliver Sacks

"What are your dreams?"

This is one of the most intimate questions a person can ask. I must have a long-term, established spiritual trust in someone before I feel comfortable answering that question. I hold my dreams airtight to my chest, hermetically sealed within the folds of my heart. Only a deep trust, built over time, will open me up. A trust that this person will not go blabbing my dreams around town, mock them, discourage, or diminish them. They will take my dreams into their own heart and shield them.

When a soul is brave enough to jump from one dream to the next, it forms the winding path of an adventurous and fulfilled life. Dreams unfold in chronological order and stack neatly on top of each other.

A dream pulls at you. Bothers you. Annoys you. Dreams will not let you rest. God planted this dream in your heart, so it will not stop nudging you until it is done. This is the reason I am so happy when a dream comes true. I can rest for a little. The Chapters of the Fathers backs this up. Rabbi Tarfon says, "U'Baal Ha'Bayis Dochek." The Master of the House will keep knocking.

Dreams are strange, specific, and different for everyone. No two people have the same dream sequence. A persistent pull of the heart tells you that it is time for a new dream to start. This relentless beckoning feeling is how you know.

It is important to know one thing: You did not give yourself this dream. Therefore, it is not yours to carry alone. God loves to step inside your dreams and work alongside you. So dream BIG, bigger than your particular skill set. The exact moment when your dream surpasses the confines of your specific talents and capabilities, chuck it into the hands of God for Him to take over. He has a whole squadron of angels waiting to be dispatched.

Life Coach Mastin Kipp asks, "Why do we set a goal?" He brilliantly answers, "We set goals not only for the goal itself, but to FEEL the emotion that goal will bring us."

So what is this emotion that I feel when I arrive on the other side of a dream? The most divine emotion possible: Satisfaction of having Co-Created with God.

I partnered up with God and we brought forth something amazing into creation. I have never felt a more exhilarating type of euphoria than this. I want to open the secret vault of my heart to you and share some of the dreams God built into my soul:

- To be accomplished
- To feel beautiful
- To get married
- To have babies
- To have emotional intimacy with my husband

- To be adored by my husband
- To have financial freedom
- To have a home that can house guests easily
- To have my own dental practice
- To own the building for my practice
- To write a wildly successful book
- To move to Israel
- To practice dentistry in Israel
- To be a spiritual healer with intuitive abilities
- To help people become less afraid of death
- To burn incense at the Holy Temple in Jerusalem
- To live in a fifth dimensional world of love, peace, harmony, and excitement

My dreams outline the shadowy silhouette of my destiny. And form the body of my life.

Dreams require four things: heart + brain + body + soul.

- Your Heart's joyful state
- Your Brain's powerful imagination
- Your Body's relaxed actions
- Your Soul's solid trust in God.

These four elements combine to materialize the spiritual into the physical.

Dreams are worth dreaming for one simple reason. When they come true, there is no better feeling than living inside the reality you had longed for, tried for, and

Gila Jedwab

that The Divine made happen. The sweet space of Divine Fruition. The euphoria of living in tandem with God. My strange inner plan somehow matched up with His and here we are. There is not even a word for that emotion.

Whenever we weave TRUST IN GOD into the fabric of a dream, the dream arrives with God sewn into the lining. There is one big challenge with dreams. A surprisingly short amount of time will pass, probably less than a year, and your dream will devolve into something else entirely. Your new normal. The shiny coat wears off and the dream you held inside your imagination for so long is now your brick and mortar. When the novelty inevitably wears off and the responsibility that comes with the new dream (the bills, the crying baby, the tooth fixing) hits you square in the face, it is important to do one thing. Remember the feeling.

What feeling? The sublime feeling that you co-created something with The Holy One. And it was Good. Your powerful mind, heart, body, and soul joined forces and materialized here on earth an item from your vibrational vortex in heaven (Esther Hicks). You dreamed it, longed for it, God okayed it and here it is.

Intentionally dipping back into this magical feeling of co-creation with God, remembering that He is your silent partner, will lighten up any heavy drudgery involved in the day-to-day operation of your dream. Tap into this alchemy that you can now claim for yourself. You did it. You figured out the magic: how to make a dream come true. Use your newly gained intuitive skills and repeat. Get better at it. Dip your toe into the euphoric gratitude, trust, and wonder this creation of yours will always hold inside of it and use that feeling to do it all over again.

The Secret to dreams is conjuring a mental picture of your dream inside your head and then feeling, *really feeling*, how that mental picture stirs up orgasmic excitement inside your heart. The Universe loves to play a match-up game of the reality inside your head to the one in front of your eyes. The Universe wants to keep that vibration going.

Dream it, Feel it, Do it, Trust it, and then **let it go**. The letting go is the vital fifth step. Let go and be amused at the surprising ways God will deliver your dream. He always adds upgrades to the dream if you let Him. If you hold tight to one specific way, you handcuff God. If you are flexible with God, He is flexible with you. Let Him bring your dream however and whenever He wants.

Which brings me to another important concept explained best by Wayne Dyer, *Infinite Patience*.

Infinite patience is the belief that your dream will arrive on God's schedule, in Divine Time. Wayne says to let go of "the when and the how." Once you release all the whens and hows that cause worry and rumination, you clear a path for God to get to work. Your main job is to be present and receptive to the things that God is waving in front of your face, in Real Time.

Moses had many options in dealing with the burning bush. He could have panicked and doused the bush with water, without ever realizing that it was not being consumed. That probably would have been me. He also could have been daydreaming, lost in thought, and walked right past it. He could have seen it, shrugged it off, and let the next shepherd deal with it.

Instead, he remained present and engaged. Moses was curious about it. This was the reason he noticed the miracle.

The scripture says, "And Moses *turned toward* the bush." Ever see a dog turn its head sideways in curiosity? That turning comes from a calm state of curious Presence. The kind of Presence that can only originate from the soul.

When he saw the burning bush, Moses was calm. He coolly says to himself, "Asurah Nah, Let me *turn to this*." God reciprocates this same calm attention back to Moses in the next verse. It says, "Va'yare Hashem Ki Sar Lir'os." "God *saw* that Moses *turned to see*." (My emphasis.)

God took note that Moses used his soul as an instrument of curiosity instead of fear. And because of this, God immediately called out to him with love, twice, "Moses, Moses." Redundancy is the immediately discernible love language of God. Moses lent his calm Presence to his surroundings, and God reciprocated in kind —with His own presence. At the burning bush, God gives Moses (a natural introvert and loner) the daunting and outright humiliating task of going to Pharoah to try and get his Jewish brothers out of slavery in Egypt. At that point, Moses probably wished he had just kept walking past the bush.

Moses balks at God's request. He imagines the pushback and cynicism he will get from his fellow Jews. Their incredulity most likely sounded like this in Moses' head: "Let me get this right. *God appeared to you inside a burning bush and spoke to you?* After 210 years of slavery, how exactly is this plan going to work?"

Moses then asks God an interesting question: "What name of Yours should I use when they ask why they should believe me?" It is actually a great question. Moses is wondering how he can transmit his legitimacy and confer confidence to the Jewish people at the same time?

What name can accomplish all that? What name can snap Moses and the Jewish people out of their deep anxiety and turn it into belief? The name that God chooses is an interesting one. God calls Himself by the following amorphous name: "I will be as I will be." Meaning, trust me. Do not micromanage Me. You do not need to know all the details in advance, let me surprise you. Maybe try to enjoy it. This is the way all good redemption stories should go. The way all good dreams go.

Surrender is all the magic you need to watch it unfold, easily. King David offers additional vibrational advice on how to have dreams come true. "And Relish in the Lord and He will give you your heart's desires (Psalms 37;4)." This is a massive emotional clue. There exists ONE magical and mysterious emotion that can unlock the door to all our dreams. What is it??

RELISHING IN GOD!

As we get good at feeling, actually *feeling*, Relishment in God, we can sit back in awe and watch Him hand-deliver our dreams right to our doorstep. Why? Because all God wants is to keep that relicious thing going.

So, how can we relish God more, practically speaking? Sink your heart into the moment. Pay attention to whatever is front of you. Remember to filter life through the calm eyes of your soul. Rotate the wheels of your awareness outward.

Awareness turned inward brings depression, anxiety, and self-pity. Awareness turned outward brings gratitude, wonder, and peace. Become the "peaceful perceiver" of your life, says Eckhart Tolle.

In our haste, anxiety, or general preoccupation with stupidity, we can miss the whisper of God in our ear. Pay curious attention to whatever the Moment of Now is presenting you. Because that is God. When it comes to the past: reminisce it, forgive it, learn from it. When it comes to the future: plan it, hope for it, contemplate it. But for the love of God, immerse yourself in the present as much as possible. Engage your soul in this here moment. Whenever you are present, that is your soul paying attention. It has come up to the surface to look around.

When my 10-year lease expired on my rented office space, I needed to think about renewing the lease. A dream buried inside started poking at me again. To own my own building. After negotiations with our landlords left me feeling frustrated, my husband and I started driving around the neighborhood looking for a building for sale. Nothing turned up. We asked a realtor to help us look, and I also asked friends. Nothing.

A little while later, we went away for a weekend Bar Mitzvah in upstate New York. We were schmoozing with our friend, Jason, a photographer. He mentioned he had recently sold his building. We asked him if he knew of anything available. He casually suggested we call our mutual friend, Jon, who owns a lot of properties in the area. I called Jon later that week. He said yes, he did have a building he is thinking of selling. We set up a meeting for Sunday. A few hours before the meeting,

The Center of All Things

Jon randomly crossed the street in front of my car as I was on my way to pick up pizza. I had never seen him on the street before. The visual image of his face shrunk down and jumped into my third eye similar to the circle that pops on my phone screen from a Facebook message. I took it as a sign.

Later that day, we met up. The building he showed us was awful. Bad location, no parking, and falling apart. I was crestfallen. The subsequent words escaped my mouth without any permission: "Do you have anything else you could show us?" He paused and replied, "I have this other building on Spruce that I wasn't really planning on selling, but I can take you over there to look at it."

The second I saw it, I felt something.

Perfect size, perfect location, perfect parking. Six months later, it was ours. Jon is a hilarious and quirky guy. He curses a lot and makes me laugh. He does not conform to the rigid formality of life. The way he conducts business is super informal and fun. He taught me a lot about being real and playful that does not contradict being a savvy businesswoman. Looking back, the lightness I felt from Jon opened a Presence inside me that prompted my spontaneous question about another building. His contagious playfulness made me more receptive to guidance from the Universe. And the Universe felt it and delivered. Easily.

Jon helped me stay inside my own playful mood as he took us around the buildings and was silly with us. I remember he made some off-color jokes about gay porn. He did not take anything too seriously and was unabashedly himself. I think he is a magnet for success because he never forgot how to be playful and enjoy. He is tapped into the secret alchemy of dreams and reminded my soul how to do it too.

Chapter Eighteen
His and Hers Laughter

God allowed most biblical parents to choose the name of their baby. Except for Isaac. God insisted on that name. Why did God hijack. Abraham and Sarah's right to name their one and only baby? Abraham was the first man to look up to the stars and wonder about the existence of God. His baby would carry that singular legacy. So why is this baby named by God Himself and why the name Isaac?

What does the name, Isaac, even mean? It means, *He laughs*. It does not mean He is funny, witty, or sarcastic. Yitzchok means the act of laughter itself. Maybe God wanted to safeguard something crucial. Maybe God wanted to point out how vital the act of laughter is to our very existence.

Maybe God named this baby to teach us one thing, that laughter sustains our eternal connection to Him. Something about laughter keeps us vibrant, alive, and in the mood to look up to the heavens and be curious about Him. Maybe God wants us to use laughter to get to know Him better. To create a lifetime full of playful connection to Him. Well, this message has endured until today. There are thousands of mothers still naming their babies, Isaac. And thousands of people still remembering how important it is to laugh.

Both of Isaac's parents laughed in disbelief when they found out Isaac would be born in their old age. But only *one* of them was reprimanded by God for laughing. It was Sarah. Why did God take issue with the way she laughed? It was her tone. It was sarcastic. Both of them laughed, but Abraham had a grateful tone to his, Sarah a cynical one.

The text says, Abraham heard the news and *"fell on his face and spoke to his own heart."* I can picture the scene in my head. Abraham on the floor, rolling around like a giddy teenager, talking to his heart. Not believing his good fortune. The text paints an entirely different scenario for Sarah. Sarah did not fall on her face. No mention of the word heart. The verse says she laughed *at* herself. She glanced sideways at her old self. She caught sight of her withered body and with one eyebrow raised said, "No way, God. You gotta be kidding me – a baby from this old body?"

That is a whole different kind of laughter. It is a dry, parched, throaty laugh, with no joy in it. God confronts Sarah for this. He responds to her with the same sarcastic tone. "Ha'Yipaley Mey'Hashem Davar?" "Is there anything beyond Hashem?"

A cautionary tale. Sarah taught us the way *not* to laugh. Do not use the gift of laughter to be sharp-tongued or self-effacing with it. Abraham showed us a lighter way. Laugh towards your heart, roll over and fall on your face. Be delighted and playful with laughter. Use it for gratitude, connection and self-love.

I love to laugh hard. I remember my first hard laugh. It was in first grade. Our teacher, Rabbi Polatoff, gave out powdered jelly donuts to the class. The donuts were sitting on the edge of our desks on a white napkin with that red exit hole making us all drool. We had to wait for recess to eat them. Each kid was glancing affectionately at his donut. I noticed that Rabbi Polatoff had a smirk on his face; he was thinking something. We caught eyes and he said, only to me, "I think some of the kids are talking to their donuts."

Rabbi Polatoff

We both broke out laughing so hard with each other, I can still feel it 40 years later. I can still hear his gravelly, raspy, staccato laugh catching itself inside my memory. I can still see the gap between his two front teeth as he laughed. We had an eye to eye, soul to soul moment. We were united inside that laughter. A 7-year-old and a 50-year-old. Our hard laugh jumped the divide of our age.

I have come to realize that laughter can also jump the divide of race, gender, sexual orientation, and religion. Inside laughter, you become the same. Norman Lear, the man who produced all the best 1970's sitcoms, wrote in his *Book of Norman*, "When we laugh together, we are One; the ability to elicit that feeling of Oneness from a huge crowd, and at a whim, is an enormous power."

There is no more intimate and satisfying interaction than sharing a hard laugh with another person. It is better than sex. Have you ever watched a person hard laughing all by themselves? It is enchanting. It is a holy moment. You cannot look away. Why? You are getting to see a flash of their unguarded essence. Same thing when people sing with their eyes closed. That is their soul captivating you.

> *There is no more intimate and satisfying interaction than sharing a hard laugh with another person*

When you live in the present moment, not distracted, rushed, or anxious, you give yourself the best opportunity for laughter. You leave the door open for something to hit you funny.

God created this strange looking, strange sounding phenomenon of laughter exclusively in Homo Sapiens. No other species seems to be doing it. Maybe laughter comes to balance the burden of all that heavy thinking we are wired to do. It is called comic relief for a reason.

Tracy Morgan relates Faith to Humor.

> "Laughter is faith. When you got worry, your faith is weak. That's how strong my faith is, I ain't got no worry. When my comedy is strong, my faith is strong."

Faith helps your soul rise up to the surface. It turns out that your soul is the thing that finds stuff funny.

Laughter is the soul's relaxed reaction of the body. It is a gift when it hits.

I was driving home with my husband after finishing a 7am food shopping run in Brooklyn, two weeks before Passover. It was now 10am, three hours later, and I was starving.

I suddenly remembered that I had an old avocado in my purse. With one hand on the wheel, I rummaged around in my bag and found it. I bit the stem off like an animal in the wild and started squirting the mushy avocado directly into my mouth. From the side corner of my eye, I caught the look of horror and disgust on my husband's face. It hit me so hard. I almost crashed the car. I could not breathe. I had tears streaming down the sides of my face. I had to pull the car over on the side of Ocean Parkway not to crash. Neither one of us will ever forget that laugh. It was a moment we fell into the timeless space of laughter together. We know the intimacy it holds forever. We touch back on it sometimes to awaken the euphoric feeling held inside that memory. Josh is funny; he named it, "The time I mainlined an avocado."

In addition to feeling so good, laughter is also the herald for healing. When you suddenly find that you are able to crack a weak smile about something that used to sting your heart so badly, you know you are getting somewhere. Inside of us lives that 5-year-old who remembers how to be silly and laugh. How to playhouse and clink glasses at a tea party. How to tilt your head sideways at clouds and birds and other people with wonder instead of judgement. There is an endless reserve of raw wonder all around us. A confined and hunted Ann Frank looked out her cramped attic window and said, "When I look to the sky, I feel that everything can change for the better." That kind of unbridled, untamed wonder safeguards optimism and hope under even the worst of circumstances.

To live with a heart full of wonder, playfulness, and flirtation is to be irresistible to the world around you. Remember as often as possible that we are here for a short ride and to laugh.

The times I am most proud of myself as a mother are the times I played with my kids. Went into the fake houses they built. Ate the fake food they made with tiny utensils. Took the invisible food to my lips and chewed it noisily, purring at how delicious it was, always asking for more.

> *To live with a heart full of wonder, playfulness, and flirtation is to be irresistible to the world around you*

If there was an amusement ride outside a supermarket, I always put a quarter in and threw them on. I know for sure that these things made me good as a mother, the times I went inside their playful world with them.

Be playful with God too. Shake your head in amused delight at the lengths God will go to flirt with you. Signs, symbols, and coincidences that God orchestrates for our specific entertainment. He flirts with all of us, all the time. There is so much breathless intimacy and wide-eyed shock in the spontaneous synchronicity He brings me. When God bats his larger-than-life eyelashes at me, I glance around to see if anyone else is watching.

Flirtation is an amazing jolt of caffeine. It perks up my nodding head and makes my heartbeat faster. It is the spiciest ingredient of the best marriages. When my husband flirts with me, I stop whatever I am doing. God keeps this world from being too serious. Have you ever seen the goofy smile on the underside of a saw-nose shark or heard the ridiculous honk of a sloth? God has an unexpected sense of humor. It is the plot twist, the being caught off guard, that makes us laugh the hardest.

The night Donald Trump got elected is a perfect example of God's hilarity. All I could do at 3am on that euphoric night was roll around on my bed and say to my heart, "Hashem, you are funny. You chose this unexpected man to get the world spinning in the right direction again, to be the seismic shift we needed. I can't thank You enough."

Chapter Nineteen

Torah

When I live with a Real God, and talk to Him in Real Time, He uncovers something special for me. I see the Torah scroll stand up, twist and stretch, and shake off its 3000-year-old dust right before my eyes. The people inside that book come to life and morph into relatable human beings. The Bible transforms from the oppressive rule book handed to me in high school, to an adult fascination. I scour the text for hints He drops at me, left and right. I can visualize the people inside with eyebrows and toenails (that all need some trimming).

I ride the roller coaster of emotions with them. I feel myself inside their colossal mistakes and their earnest striving. I feel amused, delighted, confused, and intrigued by their odd behavior. I choke up when they cry, especially that time Yosef had to run to another room to cry by himself. Been there. I have picked up clues from them on how to have a Real Relationship with God, which includes the following elements.

REAL CONVERSATION:

Moses, a man who spoke directly to the FACE OF GOD, was like, "No, please no, not me, God, pick someone else. I talk funny." He resisted God's request to go save the Jewish people at least six times!

Moshe was *face to face* with God and still doubted himself and *still argued*. If this is not the ultimate precedent for a genuine relationship with God, what else is? If these conversations, recorded for eternal posterity in the Bible, do not demonstrate that God invites us to be Real and feisty with Him, nothing does. We witness from Moses that we can confide how we truly feel, we do not have to pretend to be something we are not, and God will meet us right where we are, inside our fears and insecurities. He will help us troubleshoot a solution. Just like He did with Moses, He got Aaron on board to help do the talking for his brother.

MISTAKES:

Abraham, the Forefather of Faith and Trust in God, LIED to Pharaoh about who his wife was, twice! Because he was afraid. Many people in the Bible had favorite wives and favorite kids and all the things that make me want to cringe. When they went down to Egypt during the famine, Jacob came across super ungrateful and complaining when Pharaoh asked him how he was doing. There may be deeper explanations for their behavior, but at the surface, their mistakes appear human and relatable and I see myself inside them. No one is perfect. This loosens the noose of self-condemnation and judgement. I realize that we all make mistakes. Once free, I can climb up the next rung on the character ladder: Admitting my mistakes.

My favorite dental education course is the one where the dentist shows slides of his epic failures. I want to jump over the table, run to the stage and hug him at that point.

A mistake admitter is my favorite kind of person. They invite me to lay down my own ego and drop the pretense of perfection. It is one of the most ego-dissolving experiences. Show me your mistakes, I will show you mine, and we can be friends forever.

Whenever I make a mistake, I try to catch myself and then immediately do these five things: Tell God about it, apologize to whomever I wronged, figure out why I messed up, figure out how to do better next time, and move on. I apologize like this to my kids so they can learn the technique and because kids deserve apologies all the time. They are the most discriminated against and dismissed population on the planet.

When I was a young mother in my early twenties, I was also in dental school. I was sleep-deprived and mostly raising our kids alone. My husband was in medical school two hours away from my dental school, so we lived apart during the week. I was in survival mode and did not even know it. My baby was crying in the middle of the night, and I stumbled into her room, exhausted. She had vomited over the side of her crib, all over the carpet. She was a career vomiter. In my delirium, I pulled her out of the crib and sat her in the corner of the room. I scrubbed the carpet clean. I wiped her up and put her back in the crib and let her cry herself back to sleep.

The next day she woke up with a fever. I ran her to the doctor. She had strep throat. I carried the guilt of that night for 16 years. That I let my sick baby cry herself to sleep alone. I put her in the corner to cry alone, because I was more worried about the mess. It made me feel like a monster. Sixteen years later, with a trembling heart and voice, I sat with my daughter at our dining room table and told her about that night. I asked her if she could forgive me. She looked at me so softly and sweetly and said, "Of course, Mommy. I totally forgive you. I understand that you were exhausted." In one moment, she released me from my guilt prison of 16 years.

Admitting mistakes is hard. It is nullifying. It is also the best gift you can give yourself. Admitting a mistake clears out the attic of your soul. There is no reason to hoard your guilt and shame.

Admitting a mistake is like the 1(800) GOT-JUNK truck that pulls right up to your soul, backs up and hauls out those dusty boxes of guilt and shame.

COMPROMISE:

God allows Himself to be persuaded back to reason by Moshe's desperate argument not to destroy the Jewish people after the sin of the Golden Calf (Parshat Ki Sisa). Here, God models for us how to achieve a really high level of ego nullification. He shows us how to come down off a high-horse proclamation and "accept influence," as John Gottman named it. God backed Himself into a corner with His declaration of destroying the Jewish people, but then allowed Himself to be coaxed back to reason by Moshe, a human being. God opened His heart back up after a burst of rage. We can learn a lot from that. It is never too late to soften, to listen to compromise, and to back-track.

I ask myself, what else was God trying to teach me here? That He wants real argument and real engagement, like Moshe gave. He wants me to use my authentic voice, not my glaze-eyed, zombie, submission voice.

God displays the other side of that heated interaction. How to be humble in an argument, how to lay down arrogance, hear the other person's voice, and acquiesce. These are the skills necessary for healthy interplay inside a relationship: to have a strong voice of your own while still leaving space to hear the voice of the other. There are so many relational skills inside the Torah that psychologists are first formulating a modern, scientific language for and writing entire books about.

HUMANNESS:

When Rivka and Rachel first met their men, their first instinct was to run and tell their parents. The text highlights that they *ran*. Something any young girl who just met their love would do. The language of the text lends permission to be the playful and excitable human beings that God created us to be. To honor that irrepressible human spirit bubbling within us.

ACCEPTING ADVICE:

Moshe heeded the unsolicited advice of his father-in-law, Yisro, when he was overwhelmed by all the inquiries of the nation. He could not see a solution to the problem because he could not even see that there was a problem, *because he was inside the problem*.

Lesson: When you are inside a problem, the problem is so close to your nose that your vision gets obscured. Moshe needed the outside perspective of someone he trusted, who was brave enough to approach him and tell him there was a problem.

I learn from this not to be stubborn, to allow for someone that may know better than me to approach me, to advise me on a Blindspot Issue. Even if that person is one of my in-laws. God used the most extreme example.

HUMILITY VS EGO:

Whenever God is fed up with the Jewish people in the Bible, He reaches over and over for the same stinging insult, "A stubborn, stiff-necked people." Ouch. If stubbornness is the worst insult God can hurl at us from His vast lexicon, it must be bad.

Humility, on the other hand, is the singular compliment God reaches for to describe Moses when he chooses him to lead. If humility is the greatest compliment and stiff-necked the worst, they must be opposites. Humility means being alive with the realization that all you are and all you achieve is **from** God and **for** God. Humility looks like someone giving every inch of the Glory to God.

A neck turns stiff when the Ego holds tight to a situation or outcome and does not allow room for God to do His work. The Ego wants to either complain or take credit for itself. The Ego seeks its own honor and stiffens the neck. The Ego will not turn right or left to see the miracles that God is eager to provide.

The Ego does not know how to be easy with the situation and trust the Higher Power. The Ego always delivers on its acronym, it always knows how to Edge God Out. Our main job is to Edge God Out. Our

> *Humility is like yoga: it stretches out your soul to become more flexible*

main job is to acknowledge the Ego inside and shrink it down to a manageable size.

Humility is like yoga: it stretches out your soul to become more flexible. Humility places God At The Center (GATC) of all things. Humility frees the psyche from the external burden to please-people. With God At The Center, the opinions of other people drop by the wayside. Insults hurt a lot less when you put the feelings of God first. It is no longer about your honor, it is about His.

Moses understood that God was everything. And God understood that He was at the Center of Moses' heart. Because of his selfless motivation, Moses had free reign to speak Truth to God's Power. God calls Moses His *most faithful and most humble servant.* Moses shows us what that looks like. A faithful servant is not meek and submissive. He is the servant who speaks up and tells you the truth. He is the servant who guards your best interest and calls you out when you need to hear it. Moses uses his stubbornness and ego for only one thing, the sake of God's honor. Moses feared that God would look weak in the eyes of the Egyptians.

Moses was the only prophet to merit a crystal clear, face to face relationship with God. Why? Because Moses was in the game ONLY for God. Moses had a chance to prove this. When? When God wanted to destroy the Jews after the Sin of the Golden Calf and start a new nation over with Moses. Moses replied with the most humble answer possible. He asked to have his name erased from the Bible. (Exodus 32:32) Anyone else's Ego would have perked up at that offer. "A brand new nation starting from me?" Hmmm.

Moses was only ever worried about one thing, the reputation of God. Later in the Bible, after the Sin of the Spies, Moshe immediately argues, "If you destroy the Jews, what will the Egyptians say?" They will say that God could not deliver His people to their land. The thought of them maligning God devastated Moses. The argument that emerged from Moses was like a reflex of humility. No part of this was about Moses seeking a legacy. His only concern was God's reputation. Why was Moses the only prophet to merit this unique closeness? Maybe because Moses was the first prophet to figure out the REAL Secret.

The Real Secret being this:

The more REAL we deal with God, the more REAL He will appear to us. If we act as if He is standing right in front of us, He will actually stand right in front of us.

So then the practice of humility becomes simple. It boils down to some easily implementable questions:

1. Do I feel Him breathing inside me?

2. Do I feel God as REAL inside my heart?

3. Is He at the Center of my thoughts and motivation?

4. Do I put His Glory and His Honor before my own?

5. Do I remember and trust that He is running the show?

6. Can I let go of the need to try to control life, both mine and other peoples?

When you are mindful of these questions, they help you relax that stiff neck we had back in the Bible. Humility is a muscle relaxant that helps us swivel our neck in all directions, especially up. Our collective practice of humility and spiritual flexibility will attract more of God's Real presence down into our Reality.

HEART:

In Parshat Vayakhel, when the Jewish people are given instructions to build the Mishkan, (The Tabernacle) God's Home on earth, God uses one particular adjective 14 different times. God uses the word *Heart*. God exclusively sought *wisdom of the heart* and *donations of the heart*. Any participation in the process of building God a home had to be filtered through the heart, for the simple reason that anything passed through the heart comes out the other side with authenticity and connection.

God wanted his Home built on that energy.

HIS NAME:

I used to be baffled by the prayer of Shema. Six ordinary words that every Jew knows by heart. These words felt too short and anticlimactic to me.

"Hear O' Israel, Hashem is our God."

Strong start. Heart beating. Some big announcement coming. Trumpets are ready. Then the next three words,

"Hashem is One."

Wait, what, that is it? That was the big declaration? I am not even sure what that means or why that is the life-altering message God gathered our collective attention to hear. How exactly are we One? What does that concept even mean?

Then I analyzed the words a little differently and I saw something new.

HaShem literally means "The Name." God is universally called The Name by most Jews. Maybe this comes to teach us something about names.

We become One inside his Name. **Ha***shem* **Echad**, it is literally ***the name*** that makes us **One**.

Calling out to God by His name gives each of us a mutual starting point into the relationship with Him. We name babies and dogs and motorcycles because it is *through the name* that we gain entry to the relationship. When you begin to think about anyone in your life, you pull them to your consciousness through their name. Try it.

UNITY:

God gave us 72 names to work with. We have all kinds of nicknames and terms of endearment for Him. He gave us plenty of options. Whichever name we choose, whenever we use it to call to Him, we become One with anyone who came before to have done that.

We become one unified forcefield inside the calling of His name. As if we all chose the same woman to call Mom or Mommy or Mama or Mum. Each one who calls to her is a sibling to the other. Calling a loved one by a common name creates a funnel of kinship.

The common names we are all calling God echo inside that funnel and unites humanity as ONE family.

Norman Lear helped me understand another way we are all One. He said, "Each person is just a different version of you." He slid this concept home for me.

We are all offshoots of the giant ONE. I look at Shaquille O'Neal and think that guy is just another version of me, and I feel instant kinship and affection for him. Our outsides look so different, but on the inside, we totally match.

When that thought sinks in, I cheer for people instead of competing with them. I am One with them because that person is just another me living inside a different skin. There is no other. Everyone's talent is my talent, everyone's success is my success, their beauty is my beauty.

On the flip side, whatever struggle a person is facing, I see him as "Taking it for the team." I am grateful this soul agreed to endure the challenge for the sake of the collective. This expansive perspective stretches the elastic muscle of my heart to a size that can accommodate the whole world.

The owner of a jewelry store in the Old City of Jerusalem once told me something I will never forget. He told me that he used to be a history teacher. When he taught his students the history of the Holocaust, one thing always stood out to him. He said Survivors witnessed and documented that when the Nazis would hear the Jews cry out Shema right before they were killed, the Nazis would become momentarily terror-stricken. Maybe those six words awakened a terrifying empathy inside them, reminding their subconscious for a split second that we are all One. When you harm one, you harm all. When you help one, you help all.

ONGOING COLLABORATION:

In the beginning, while God was creating the world, certain verbs started popping up. He hovered, He spoke, He called by name, He made, He separated, He blessed. He did this fun work of creation *All by Himself*.

Then, on the 6th day, when God decided to make man. He took a huge risk. God turned to the angels and said, "Let **us** make man." This is the first plural verb used in the Bible. God left Himself wide open to the colossal misinterpretation that there may be more than one of Him. Why would He take that risk? Maybe to show us that creating by yourself can be fun for a while but when you get to the really good stuff, like making a human being, collaboration is way better. Maybe the words "Let Us" are still in effect today. Maybe all of us are contributing to the ongoing collaboration of mankind, adding moment by moment, to the evolution of human consciousness in real time. Or… Maybe God was talking to the Galactic Federation of Light (Lori Ladd). Here is to hoping we find out soon.

WORDING

As each scene of life passes before our eyes, the language we select to narrate the on-going script to ourselves, our inner running-commentary can accomplish one of two things:

Bring you pain or bring you comfort. That is it. If you find yourself swimming in a sea of pain, how can you throw yourself a rope? EDIT THE SCRIPT! NARRATE THE PLOT WITH DIFFERENT WORDS!CHANGE THE STORYLINE! The individual words we tell ourselves about any event **becomes** the way we feel about it. Search out *different words* until you find ones that soothe you. If I am sad, I sort through the words in my head and locate those little buggers causing the negative emotion. Then I rifle around my mental Rolodex until I find better words. *All is well. Life is easy.* Or I search my mind for mental snapshots of past euphoric events, like vacations, births, or reunions to dip back in and revive good feelings inside.

The ultimate example of poor choice in wording is the word, Death. Death is the worst word for death. The minute I use a different word for death I feel better about it.

Sometimes I replace it with, "He slipped back over to the other side" or "She went back home." Esther Hicks likes to say about her husband Jerry, that "He croaked." She wants to remind us that death is just the re-emergence into pure positive energy. And while croaking feels hard to those still left on this side of mixed, chaotic energy, for those who have jumped back over to the other side, it is only bliss. They have traded in this heavy, 3-dimensional body in for a lighter body. All the heavy emotions have been switched for lighter ones. Death is the best vehicle-upgrade.

One big script flip for me is this: I try never to speak of those who jumped back over in the past tense. Speaking of them in the past tense feels painful to me and, I imagine, insulting to them. I mean, they are still right here, we just cannot see them. It is *our* problem.

Speaking in present tense about dead people sounds weird, so I do not do this too often. I conform to the standard past tense wording most of the time. But to myself and in the company of people who know how weird I am, I will always talk about those who have slipped over in the Present Tense. This accomplishes three things:

Present Tense keeps them alive for me and, more importantly, keeps the relationship going.

Present Tense makes their croaking feel a lot less painful. Present Tense gives me a right now with them plus a future to look forward to with them.

Present Tense keeps them current, so whenever it is that we do get back together, we will be able to pick up right where we left off. The relationship may feel a little one-sided for now (like our relationship with God). But loved ones on the other side will find ways of letting you know they are here. My Bubby sends me red birds all the time.

Talking to them like they are sitting right next to you is the best balm for soothing the aching grief of missing them. There are no police coming to arrest you for having a full conversation with a dead person. You can be as crazy as you want, it is your mind. Sometimes, I soothe myself with sensory reminders of my croaked loved ones. For example, I will sink my face into a towel drenched in the aroma of mothballs to get a strong hit of my Bubby. Smell transports me right back to her kitchen table, right next to her.

Another trick to shift emotions with language is to add the word DIVINE to anything you are worrying about. *All things in life happen in Divine Time and with Divine Coordination and Divine Guidance.* This one-word cuts anxiety in half for me, every time. I learned this skill from my Divine Therapist, Stephanie.

Do not call them Ten Commandments.

Call them Ten Utterances. Or Ten Suggestions.

Which is a more accurate translation of the Hebrew word, *Dibrot*, anyway. God uttered them to us — as a favor. They were not commanded. They were written down by God as an opportunity for our personal development and as Ten separate portals of connection to Him. The ten commandments are essentially God's Ten goals for the world that He happened to jot down.

Which teaches us something important about writing down our own goals.

A Harvard study on the effect of writing down goals showed three groups:

The First Group (84%) had no goals.

The Second Group (13%) had goals that were not written down.

The Third Group (3%) had goals that were written down.

The second group earned 2X that of the first.

The third group earned 10X the two other groups combined.

This is how much success God wanted with his Ten Utterances. He wrote them in stone. Twice.

The best twist I have seen with wording came from a 75-year-old patient of mine. He told me his girlfriend was waiting for him out in the waiting room. Like a stealth ninja, I slowly rolled my chair over and peeked my head around the wall.

There sat his 80-year-old wife of over 50 years, casually thumbing through a magazine. This guy changed the game for me. I started to say *husband* when I wanted to feel security and pride. And I switch over to *boyfriend* when I want to feel the butterflies, flirt, and excitement. Words have that much power.

TRUTH and VULNERABILITY

"The Truth is like a lion, you don't have to defend it. Let it loose; it will defend itself."— St. Augustine

This captures how I feel about the State of Israel. We do not need this massive effort of defending the truth of the land of Israel to the world. The truth is built into Israel's walls and walks its earth. Every footstep whispers, *the Jewish people belong here.*

This truth does not need 500 Jewish lawyers defending it. We can go back to the rest of our business, confident that this truth will handle itself. Truth walks a confident stride. It does not have to repeat itself ten times or raise its voice. Truth is a clean fire that can consume a thicket of overgrown lies.

In most Jewish prayers, wherever Truth is mentioned, Kindness immediately follows. They go hand in hand. They do their best work in tandem. Kindness tempers Truth, and Truth tempers Kindness. They balance each other out. The sharp edges of Truth become rounded when spoken in Kindness. And cloyingly sweet Kindness finds balance through a fresh squeeze of Truth. Truth sprinkles just the right amount of salt onto Kindness.

Terry Real, a master on relationships, alludes to this saltiness in one of his books, *New Rules*: "The most reliable long term sexual stimulant is the ability to be truthful." (pg. 124). That is how powerfully provocative Truth is to our soul.

However, Terry is not a big fan of Unbridled Truth, as he calls it. We must take the pause to let the "woosh" pass, as Terry advises, and let our emotions organize around Kindness before launching into Truth. We innately understand the harsh cruelty of Unbridled Truth, but not many people speak of the hidden and latent cruelty of Unbridled Kindness.

What does Unbridled Kindness look like?

It looks like the family member bringing more fried chicken and grits to the obese person in bed, on the show *My 600 Pound Life*. Unbridled Kindness also goes by another name, Enabling.

Enabling is giving in to another person's fears or demands in order to avoid one thing—the uncomfortable confrontation that comes along with Truth Telling.

Unbridled Kindness also looks like 'protecting' the elderly in nursing homes from family visits during coronavirus. The elderly withered, became depressed, lonely, and isolated. Unbridled Kindness looks like a classroom of first graders sitting apart from each other, wearing masks over their little innocent faces, made to carry the misplaced burden and responsibility of life and death. True Kindness does not carry the energy of guilt, shame, intimidation, or bullying. Once 'Kindness' has been universally imposed or mandated, you need to call it something else.

Kindness needs Truth at its core to remain authentic. Kindness without a solid core of Truth stabilizing the center, slumps over. Kindness becomes horribly misshapen. During Coronavirus, when Truth went missing from Kindness, we found ourselves in a lopsided world that only Truth can set straight.

What does Unbridled Truth look like?

It looks like Gordon Ramsey yelling like a lunatic on Hell's Kitchen. (Although he has softened up a little over the years.) Truth is best served in a soft wrap of Kindness.

Esther Perel gives a great guideline: "Know what needs to be said, and what needs to not be said. Or, what needs to be said, but maybe to somebody else. Understand when honesty as confession is caring, and when it is cruel." Review your truth in your head. Use your best skill of empathy to imagine how your truth will be received inside the heart of the other person. Will it create more connection or more disconnection? How can you deliver your truth so the other person can receive it as the gift of love and connection you intend it to be?

Truth, for the sake of connection, is one of the bravest acts we can do. It means having the guts to look someone in the eyes, with all the kindness and connection we can muster, and tell them the God's Honest Truth. There is an immediate somatic relief hearing the Truth brings, even if it hurts. Your soul always turns in the direction of Truth. Your soul recognizes the frequency

> *True Kindness does not carry the energy of guilt, shame, intimidation, or bullying*

of Truth as soon as it hears it. The vibration of Truth excites your electrons.

Truth whistles with clarity. Truth enters the ear in a fresh way and perks up the soul. When the soul hears the Truth, it says, "Ah, there's the Truth. Now we can really know each other, without all the static in the way." Truth not only crumbles down a brick wall, it also clears away the rubble.

When God repeatedly calls the Jewish people a "stubborn, stiff-necked people," He is not doing this to insult us. He is trying to tell us the Truth. So, we can take a hard look at ourselves and make some changes. Unfortunately, stubbornness is a difficult barrier to penetrate. (Ask me how I know!) Truth is your best chance of getting through.

Truth is hard to muster, and hard to express. Truth takes courage. Why is that? The answer is simple. Truth creates change and people are afraid of change. People who are terrified to tell the Truth are the same people who are ghosting you in text. The Truth stays stuck in their throat. Withholding the Truth and replacing it with silence is the opposite of kindness. It is cruel and crazy making. Silence is the easier way to slip out of a situation, but it is the coward's way out.

People withhold the Truth for another reason. They are afraid of losing people to the Truth. Because the Truth hurts feelings. This is true, Truth can hurt, but only in the short game. Truth always has the long game in mind. Truth keeps the soul steadily on course. Truth navigates and steers life from the wider bird's-eye view of the soul.

> *Truth Takes Courage*

I heard Tony Robbins admit in an interview that he knew marrying his first wife was a mistake. So why did he go along with it? He said, "As silly as it sounds now, I didn't want to hurt her feelings."

Tony revealed his Truth about that situation. In his brave admission, he gives others the courage to speak their own Truth. He is attempting to spare the rest of us the same pain by bravely sharing his personal story. There is always silent anguish and inevitable backtracking that goes along with a prolonged withholding of your Truth. *Speaking the Truth fast tracks you to your destiny.*

Imagine the suffering Tony could have spared his first wife had he told her the painful truth before the wedding. Holding back his Truth sunk him deeper in the hole. The longer he withheld the Truth, the harder it became to climb out. Tony used his own hard-earned lessons, in the highest way possible, to teach the rest of us about Truth. To bravely move us forward.

Martha Beck concurs. She said, "Nothing feels better to the soul than the truth." How right she is. Truth is a blessed relief. Truth is a glowing crystal inside a dark cave. It helps you assess your surroundings, get your bearings, and get the hell out.

What is the powerful force embedded inside Truth? Truth is a magic pill that dissolves confusion. A mental clarity arises from ingesting truth. Truth shows you exactly where you stand. You can plant your feet on the firm ground of Truth and slowly walk towards something or away from something. Without Truth, you are left to wander and spin. Truth lights up your next move. Truth creates a whirlwind of energy and movement, enough to get your legs unstuck. (Stephanie) I experienced the absolute miracle of Truth-Telling firsthand. Truth-Telling took down the highest wall in my life. I was lying in bed one night, in the snore room off my bedroom. The one I escape to whenever my husband's snoring gets too loud. I was lying restlessly on my back, awake and agitated, in a state of despair, struggle, and loneliness. I had just experienced a rejection from someone who hurt me to my core. I was not yet in an intimate soul space with my husband. We were good friends raising kids together, living parallel lives. I was mostly walking on eggshells around him to keep the peace for 21 years. On this night, for reasons I cannot explain, a specific piece of Truth hidden inside my heart was banging on the door to get out. It took on a life of its own. For some reason, my soul was insisting that telling my husband this Truth was the only chance I had for a real relationship with him. I was so scared, I could not even swallow.

I gathered up my courage, the kind of courage that makes my heart jump into my throat seconds before I am about to do something crazy. I walked into our bedroom and heard the familiar pattern of his snoring. I gently snuck under his covers and waited. He stirred. I swallowed hard. He woke up confused and groggy; it was midnight. I quietly said, "There is something I need to tell you." He saw my face. He softened. I clicked my Invisalign retainers out of my mouth, and inside a soft, shaking voice that I could not recognize, these words of Truth that were buried deep inside my heart since I was 16 years old found their freedom.

I fully expected him to get upset, hurt, crazed. All would be normal, proportional reactions to the truth I just told him.

Instead, something else happened.

He sat up and looked at me with the most tender eyes I have ever seen. He said a single sentence that I can still hear him say. "That must have been really hard for you." And then he held me. For the first time in 21 years, I felt something brand new from him. Instead of the jealousy or the rage or the stone-cold silence I was bracing for, I felt the arms of his human kindness reaching out in the dark to comfort me.

My Truth, delivered to him with humility and fear, caused a miracle. It cranked open the sealed 500-pound metal lid covering the vault where his soul was hiding. And his soul slipped out and comforted mine. The usual reactions of his ego were nowhere to be found. Looking back, I see what happened that night. Speaking my deepest Truth did something. It called forth the kindest version of my husband to appear on the scene. My Truth beckoned to his Kindness. My Truth delivered us a miracle. And it was a groundbreaking moment for us to begin to have something most people are missing in their married life: *real life, soul to soul, spiritual intimacy.*

We will still have hard times ahead of us. Ups and downs. But I know if I go back to this moment, it will always remind me to look for the person (soul) inside him. I knew, for the first time in our marriage, that *connection of soul* was possible with him. That is how powerful the Truth can be. Truth can crank open the rusty hatch just enough to let the waiting soul slip out. There is no greater Kindness than helping someone release the trapped parts of their soul. Fragments of their soul that went into hiding during a hostile childhood. Truth is like a detective dispatched to locate the whereabouts of missing parts of the soul.

Conventional therapy will make *no progress out of misery* unless some hard Truths are spoken by the therapist inside that room. Go and read any of Terry Real's books to understand this concept. He sums up this method of Truth-Telling with one directive. He teaches therapists to find a way to say **to** the patient the same things they would say **about** the patient to their colleagues at the water cooler. In other words, tell the patient the Truth. What a revolutionary concept in therapy!

With all the hectic madness of life, getting glimpses of the liberated soul of your partner keeps oxygen flowing inside the connection. Those glimpses remind me that there is a touchstone inside him that I can rely on to be reasonable and rational and, best of all, ever accessible. A Soul Connection that he is *willing* and *able* to share with me. A safe space I can always reach for, inside him, even during the worst argument. There can be no real intimacy without this Safety of Accessibility. A safety that comes from knowing the other person will never deny you access to their soul, no matter what life brings. Until I felt safe inside this Accessibility of Soul with my husband, I would not show him mine. I kept the accessibility of my own soul hidden and protected from him during our troubled years, when his soul was buried. Now that I feel safe with him, I show him flashes of my soul throughout the day. How? With tender, playful, loving, sustained eye contact. Spontaneous loving hugs. With words of refined truth, meaning, and substance. These are subtle ways of brushing my soul up against his. When I need a quick hit of Connection, I ask him to give me his eyes and I give him mine and we smile like goofballs at each other.

Speaking the Truth means speaking from the Soul. The only language the Soul can articulate is the Truth. As words pass through layers of Ego, they get coated with the muck of hidden agendas, subtle manipulation, and outright lies. It is our Ego that shapeshifts the Truth.

Our Soul knows something vital: When we take a minute to allow our words of Truth to organize themselves and emerge from the Soul, they swirl up a tremendous life force, like the kind I experienced that night with my husband. The energy inside spoken Truth wakes God's attention. He wants to come down and check out what just happened. God just heard you speak the Essence of Himself, The Truth, and He wants to match it with a miracle. "Truth sprouts form the earth (us humans) Justice peers down from Heaven." (Psalms 85:11) – Truth always gets God's undivided attention.

Another important point: Always tell God your plain Truth. He knows it anyway. It will create intimacy between the two of you when you confide in Him what he already knows. He is the best place to blab your messiest truth and then laugh with Him about it.

Rabbi Elimelech of Lizhensk said, "I am confident of being admitted into Gan Eden (Heaven). The heavenly court will ask me, "Melech, did you study adequately?" And I will say, "No." The court will say, "Did you pray properly?" And I will say, "No." It will say, "Did you give adequate charity?" And I will say, "No." The court will say, "He is Truthful. Let him in."

> *Speaking the Truth means speaking from the Soul*

The first agreement in Don Miguel Ruiz's book, *The Four Agreements*, is the one I never have trouble remembering. It says, "Be Impeccable with Your Word."

I love that word, "Impeccable."

It reminds me to take that moment to filter my words through my Soul. So, they come out playful, transparent, and absolutely truthful. This process wipes the muck and confusion off of them. The sludge of people-pleasing or ass-kissing or trying to present myself in a certain way slides right off. Impeccable words are squeaky clean and glistening. They perk up other Souls standing nearby.

I once walked a patient up to the front desk to schedule her next visit with me. This patient was a known offender. She cancelled appointments at the last minute or sometimes did not even show at all. Her issue: She was afraid. Now, this next visit we needed was three hours long. I felt an air of playfulness and Truthfulness come over me as we stood together at the front desk. I knew I could not stand there and pretend that everything was okay and that I was not nervous setting aside three hours of my day for her. I felt the Truth organizing itself inside.

I paused, filtered, and with a playful smirk I said, "If you wanna bail, that's fine, I totally understand. I just need three days' notice from you so we can fill the spot; otherwise, I will have to charge you a cancellation fee." We both smiled.

I did not stand there and pretend all was fine. Or that she was someone she was not. Or that I did not care if she did not show up. I addressed the situation with honesty and levity, and I think we both appreciated it. The less Truthful me would have wanted to present myself as not caring if she Did not show up.

To pretend that I was that relaxed and easygoing. But I am not. It really upsets me when people cancel at the last minute. That was a moment I felt the liberating power of being impeccable with my word. Impeccable Truth creates a lucid transparency between beings.

Speaking Truth opens into another arena of soul dexterity, the art of Vulnerability.

This is how I define **Vulnerability**:

The practice of being afraid of looking like a total idiot and doing it anyway, with the right person at the right time, for the sake of Connection.

Vulnerability comes from the Latin "Vulnus," meaning "wound." Vulnerability is the ability to share your wound or your Deep Need with another being. To open the inner vault, you normally have under 24-hour armed surveillance. When I witness another person being vulnerable, it does three surprising things: it makes me love them, it makes me trust them, and it reminds me how to do it.

Elie Wiesel was my greatest literary teacher of Vulnerability. In his book, *Night*, Elie confessed the deepest, most Vulnerable Truth about the death of his father in the concentration camp's barracks. A Truth that made him look like a monster. A Truth that made him look human. A Truth that went back and made me believe every other word he wrote.

> *Speaking Truth opens into another arena of soul dexterity, the art of Vulnerability*

Elie confessed, "His last word had been my name. He called out to me, and I had not answered...and deep inside me, if I could have searched the recesses of my feeble conscience, I might have found something like: Free at last!!..."

Whoa. Now that's a vulnerable confession.

Authors have the luxury of foisting their most naked Vulnerabilities into the ether, hoping a brave, anonymous soul out in the void will catch them. Writers who spill their bravest Truths are silently praying to be caught and embraced on the invisible plane where all human thought mingles. The most Vulnerable writers are the most successful writers. Because readers like you and me are on the prowl for one thing: to catch a glimpse of our own Vulnerability inside someone else's.

In the act of being Vulnerable, your soul swims right up to the surface. Your Ego is down; you are exposed and humble. You unbuttoned your trench coat, and you are naked under there. You are allowing your deepest flaws and wounds to be seen. Vulnerability looks different for all of us because our injuries are all so different. Your Vulnerability is specific to your life story. You can be Vulnerable about anything: your eye color, weight, sexuality, intelligence, success, foot size, hair length.

Vulnerabilities are like hidden sunburns, you guard them. You do not want anyone tapping on them. You wince at the lightest of touches and your overreaction makes no sense to other people (R' Hanoch Teller).

When our Vulnerabilities get brushed up against, even lightly, our silent alarm goes off. If someone freaks out at you for something you considered harmless, and it leaves you baffled, rest assured, you just touched their wound.

Let's say you just touched someone's Vulnerable Spot or someone touched yours, and a mini freak-out just occurred. Now what do you do? The entire trick of diffusing a Triggered Situation is to Shape-Shift. The first and most difficult step in this process is to recognize an Overreaction *as it is occurring* — in Real Time. Stop. Take a hot second to breathe and witness it. *Go absolutely still.* With awareness and with practice, we will not feel the need to escalate and react back to triggered people with our own triggered self. You can shape-shift internally and become a New Creation. A peaceful, curious Observer. You can shed your body. Float above the scene. Perceive it with curiosity. This maneuver produces the most amazing Alchemy. As you swirl your hands and change the shape of your energy from Crazed Reactor to Peaceful Witness the ticking time-bomb gets diffused. You, transformed into Peaceful Witness, lend a calm, accepting gaze that stills the triggered wound in the other and de-escalates the entire crime scene. So we can all put our guns down.

What are the gifts you receive for opening up and being Vulnerable with someone you trust?

1. You time-travel back and scoop up the injured fragments of your soul that broke off during childhood and add them back. Re-integration. You begin to feel more whole just by discussing your traumas with someone you trust.

2. You enjoy the wonderful flush of intimacy, connection, and comfort in the Now. The sweet relief of having your deepest, most embarrassing feelings shared and Accepted.

And the world did not end as you spoke them. Your soul can swell into a new fullness with Life. Someone heard your craziest stuff and still loves you.

We need to choose carefully who we are Vulnerable with, to avoid further injury to the soul. It requires a spiritually awake person on the other end. Otherwise, you risk something Brene Brown calls a Vulnerability Hangover. That horrible feeling the next morning of having been Vulnerable with someone who did not meet us there with their own wide eyes and humble soul. A person capable of listening with the empathy of their own soul catches your soul inside that safety net and completes the Vulnerability circuit.

Sometimes we take a risk. A calculated risk of being Vulnerable with someone we are not sure about, in the hopes that our Vulnerable Soul can charm their Soul up to the surface. To meet us inside that sweet space of intimacy, in the hopes of waking them up to connect with us.

We want intimacy with them so badly. Sometimes it works, sometimes it does not.

Kids are born with wide open Vulnerable Souls; they do not know any other way. If the adults in their lives do not meet, acknowledge, and cherish their exposed souls, the damage can be irreparable. The shame and confusion from offering up their innocent souls and having them be ignored, mocked, or abused, is crushing. Their souls go deep into permanent hiding from this painful injury, taking Insight and Awareness with it. They grow into beings that are all Ego, because the soul has been squirreled away for safekeeping. The hallmark symptom is that they have lost accessibility to their own Empathy, a trait that originates inside the soul. Lack of empathy is pathognomonic for a stifled soul.

In extreme cases of early childhood abuse and torture, serial killers, narcissists, and psychopaths are created. It is almost impossible to reverse that horrific kind of severe, prolonged damage to the soul.

We do not realize the lifesaving healing we do for children when we give them our Presence of Soul. To really take the time and give them a few seconds of loving eye contact. Babies, up until about age three, are eye contact gurus. They can hold prolonged eye contact, without any awkwardness, forever. They have not learned to hide their souls and avert their eyes. Their unyielding gaze instantly brings my soul up to the surface to meet theirs. Dogs are good at this too.

Vulnerability is the courage to put your fumbling heart out there in the hopes that someone will try to understand what your soul is tripping over itself to express. If the recipient is capable of steadying your soul with theirs, it brings comfort and healing. The wound begins to close with primary intention, nice, neat edges.

My therapist, Stephanie, during one of our early sessions, asked me a question that my soul was silently begging to be asked. That all of our souls are silently begging to be asked.

She asked me, "What was your primary wounding?" If we think for a minute, we all can answer this question. I sat for a minute and thought. Three people floated up to my consciousness: My parents and one of my first boyfriends.

They all, inadvertently, made me feel ugly. My parents, by giving adoring attention to my younger sister's looks and not mine. My boyfriend, by noticing and commenting on the looks of every other girl who walked by, and not mine. I mislearned early to attach my sense of worthiness or unworthiness to my looks and not to my soul. My fragile self-esteem hung itself on my face. Now that I have named and explored my wound, when people compliment my looks, I feel their innocent words touching that tender spot and I wince. I understand that not everyone has the same sensitive spot as me, but we all have something we are protecting.

When this primary wound gets triggered and I feel that familiar wincing inside my heart, I remind myself that this is my particular sunburn and that is why it hurts so much.

Mapping the landform of my own psyche, knowing where the minefields lie, helps me navigate around them. It is worthwhile to map your own inner landscape. I remember something about Terry Real's books that always bothered me. He always gave physical descriptions of the female clients in his case studies. I remember thinking how that must hurt his wife so see him describe other women as beautiful or sexy. Then I realized something HUGE. That is MY wounding and I am projecting it onto her! Maybe it does not bother her at all!

I have specific Vulnerabilities that are all smaller branches off the main injured trunk. They all have to do with appearance: my hair, my gummy smile, my

> *Mapping the landform of my own psyche, knowing where the minefields lie, helps me navigate around them*

big butt. Ironically, my sister, the beautiful one, developed an entirely different set of Vulnerabilities. She used to feel Vulnerable about her intellect. Go figure. I think her wound may have been inflicted by being taken out of class to go to The Van for extra help with learning in the early grades. Kids who got called out to The Van were made fun of.

She once told me that she was secretly afraid someone would marry her only for her looks. This was incomprehensible to me! In my parallel, deranged universe, I was *hoping* someone would marry me just for my looks! Go figure that out.

How can I heal my early wounds? Good question.

Here is my technique: The best place for healing happens inside my imagination, the playground behind my eyes. I close my eyes and enter that space.

I conjure my most nurturing, loving adult self to come forward. Then I look around for the little child that used to be me. I can always find her. I recognize her by her wide-eyed innocence. She is the one with the open heart, looking around with big, round, blue eyes, hoping to be noticed.

Hoping to be adored. She is a detective, always trying to figure everything out. I know I located my wounded inner child by the way she silently seeks. She is after one thing: Attention.

I sit her on my lap and coax her to tell the Grown Me every detail about the hurt. I bend my ear towards that hurt girl inside and listen. I squeeze her tiny body close to mine. Sometimes I just listen. Sometimes I explain to her, in simple terms, that the people did not know better, or they would have done better.

That she is perfect just the way she is. That she has everything she needs. And that God Himself created every last detail of her with His own hands. He put His most Creative Thoughts into shaping her.

I listen carefully to every word she struggles to articulate and look her steady in the eyes until she finds each one. I can give her the soul connection and curious engagement she craved back then. I travel back on the timeline of my life and nurture her in the nuanced ways she needed. I stroke her face, her hair. Tilt her chin up. Look in her eyes. I open her heart back up. I tell her to come find me anytime she needs me. I am her constant. Her rock. Her shield. I hope you can do this for your own inner child.

The Act of Vulnerability rewards both the speaker and listener. Both participants experience an opening of their heart and soul, to let in more life. The Listener gets to practice Pure Presence, by *holding space* for someone.

The Speaker receives something else. Whenever you speak about that thing that elicits a hot flash of shame inside, to the right person at the right time, you are rewarded with all kinds of Connection. You can find romance, kinship, sisterhood, and commonality. You give your pain an outlet. The breathing space it needs to heal. You hand the heavy package you were lugging around to someone you love and trust, but it's light and easy for them to take from you. And it is their absolute pleasure.

God can also be that Someone. When my pain gets triggered. When I hear a stray comment about beauty.

(My husband once called a little girl pretty and even that hurt.) I say to God, "Take it from me. Heal the deepest places inside me that I don't even have words for. Swiffer out the dusty corners of my heart that I can't reach on my own."

But be careful! Anytime someone trusts you with something Vulnerable to them, hold it tight in your hand. Never repeat it or joke about it, especially in public.

Years ago, before I understood all the rules and nuances of Vulnerability, I told my husband one of my most vulnerable things, in the hopes of connection. A few days later, he joked about it with me —loudly, within earshot of other people. I remember making a silent vow to myself to never, ever, tell him anything close to my heart again. After he woke up and I found a safe place in him, I found the language to explain to him how I felt, and he felt terrible and promised to never do that again.

DIVINE VULNERABILITY

Another huge Vulnerability of mine is talking about God enthusiastically to other people. We grew up with a lot of playful sarcasm in our house. That voice of sarcasm, still alive in my head, tries to get me to shut up when I talk too much about God. That part of me is worried that people will roll their eyes and call me ridiculous. It makes me feel like I am being too much when I do it. Like I am being silly.

So, I dampen my enthusiasm for God out of fear of ridicule, or even worse, a flat response. Writing this book was my massive effort to overcome this resistance. All creative work like art, music, or poetry, flips the contents of your innards out for public display. To a world that could criticize, trample, or worse, ignore it altogether. But the problem is, your soul will not stop nagging you until you unload its message.

So here goes.

I LOVE GOD. God is my best friend. I talk to Him whenever I am alone. I tilt my head to the right, lift my left ear to the sky. I close my eyes, point my eyeballs down, and wait for the feeling to come. The familiar tingle that starts at my left ear and shimmers its way down my left arm. I intensify this feeling with words like,

I love you Hashem. You are my hero. You are my miracle. I'm jealous of the other people who talk to you more than I do. You are my Whole Life. The one I always reach for. Stay tight to me, so I can feel you.

Intimacy with God is different from intimacy with people in one major way. We can see people, we cannot see Him. He is invisible.

This unseen relationship lives exclusively inside our imagination. We have been taught that our imagination is fake, when it actually is the most real thing we have. *Our relaxed and playful imagination births our whole life.* But the possibility exists that at the end of this, all us Believers could look like massive idiots. That is where the Vulnerability comes in. Believing in God is perhaps our greatest chance of looking like fools. (But then again, we will be dead.)

I do it anyway. Inside my quiet moments, I confide my craziest wishes, irrational fears, and deepest needs to God. I do this as plainly as I can. Without people (God)-pleasing, censoring, kissing up, bargaining, or deal-making.

Straight up. Face to face with God. I tell Him my heart, my truth, and hand over the keys. Giving Him complete control. Trusting Him to take me to amazing places, fully feeling that God guides my destiny (Psalms 16:5). I spill my heart with the singular goal of intimacy with Him. Just me and Him. He is leading me by the hand through life and I am blindfolded.

I imagine sitting inside His massive, cupped hand and letting Him fly me around to wherever He wants. I try to be all right with whatever happens, trusting that He likes adventure as much as I do. When my prayers are answered differently than I had hoped, but I continue to pray anyway, that is a whole other level of Divine Vulnerability.

God may answer me with a No or Not now. When I go with the flow and answer back, "Okay, God, Your plan, not mine." I drop my disappointment right on His lap. I keep the conversation going. I do not stiffen my neck or harden my relationship with Him. This is something I call being *loose with God*. I shake it off, stay shuckin' and jivin', and remember that He has every plant, mineral, and animal within His easy reach. If it did not happen this way, it will happen that way.

Flexibly with Faith is a holy act of Vulnerability. Believers could look like chumps at the end of this. Look at us holding tight to an invisible tetherball rope. Getting volleyed back and forth. I understand atheists: maybe deep down they are just afraid of looking like jackasses. I get it. They refuse to take this mortifying chance. Maybe they were too wounded early in life to open themselves up to this ridiculous amount of Vulnerability. They are protecting themselves from one of two things: either from devastating disappointment or from looking like a complete schmuck.

> *Flexibly with Faith is a holy act of Vulnerability*

But oh, but if they only knew the reward built into this risk. Vulnerability done right with *people* yields Intimacy. Vulnerability done right with *God* yields something ETERNALLY better.

Vulnerability with God yields Heaven here on Earth, PLUS when you get back to actual heaven, this Divine Intimacy that you grew inside your bubble of ignorance will expand in sublime ways we can only dream about. God will hold us, comfort us, nurture us in ways we cannot even fathom simply because we treated Him like He existed.

Whoever scales this formidable wall of Vulnerability with God will ultimately fall over into waiting cushions. A bouncy closeness with God equals in coziness to the risk we took of our climb being a wasted effort.

Intimacy with God grows inside the gamble we took believing in Him. The lottery payout is millions of dollars of Eternal Intimacy. The best currency in the world.

Intimacy with God is the heaven we came down here to know. We just forgot. This is one of the enormous chunks of information we are missing. Each lifetime gives another opportunity to become even more airtight with God.

Chapter Twenty

Money

We all have an inheritance about money. Every one of us. As kids, we imbibed a belief system about money from the vapors floating around our homes.

I took in a money message that went like this: there is not enough to go around and you have to work very hard for it. Most importantly, you must worry about it!

I am sure I recycled and redistributed some of this moonshine to my kids. I raised them in my twenties — the peak years of my spiritual stupidity. During my most non-woke, non-conscious, hot-mess self. Total survival mode. I hope they can feel my new and improved energy about money. I hope they can reset their money belief systems like I do every day.

Think back. What was the storyline you inherited? These are some common ones I have heard:

>Everyone is trying to rip me off.
>I have to bargain to get the best deal.
>I can't trust anyone.
>Money is hard to come by.
>There isn't enough money to go around.

I remember the paralyzing feeling. The crippling fear about money I had in the early days of our marriage. I was the one who opened all the mail and paid all the bills. I would lay restlessly in my bed at night, sunk inside worry. It was awful. I want to reach back to that younger me and help her. I wish I had possessed more soul skills back then. To know how to reach for the switch inside my mind and flip on some thoughts of trust to override the fear. To converse with God, instead of running loops around the worry track in my head.

It is crucial to examine the Operating System of your brain (Joe Dispenza) and rewrite your own code about money. Make sure to write a new program that codes for how *easily money comes to you* and *how much there is out there for all of us*.

I love the money affirmations I got from Louise Haye: "There are plenty of people out there willing to pay a good fee for the service I provide." Another Louise classic, "Money comes to me easily, from many sources, expected and unexpected."

I like to get playful about money. "Money is ridiculous. It just doesn't stop coming! It runs toward me from all directions on its tiny little money legs." Or "I reach inside my wallet and there it is. Wads and wads of cash literally jumping into my hand." I make my husband repeat them to me sometimes. He laughs. Daily repetition is crucial. *It is what you do every day that matters.* From moisturizing to meditating to flossing to rewiring old beliefs.

Repetition is a skilled locksmith; it punches the combination to open your old dusty vault. Repetition grants access to stubborn negative thoughts that got locked into your mind as a kid. Once inside that space, repetition looks around at the mess and gets to work rewriting your faulty Java script. (Bruce Lipton). I figured out a trick with repetition.

If it is with music, it is more fun. I hum to myself, "Money comes to me easily" to the tune of Happy Birthday. This lyric sneaks past the sentry guards of my old belief system, piggybacking on a song that has been there since I was three years old.

Our relationship with money sits right in our first chakra, our root chakra, near our genitals. It is that personal and that sensitive. Most people do not feel comfortable talking about it. Money talk is considered shameful, dirty, and inappropriate. Well, guess what, I love talking about it! It excites me and makes me tingle. It frees me. You cannot run a business if you cannot get comfortable speaking openly about money. No shame, no guilt — JUST JOY about money.

This is what I do with cash. I close my eyes. I picture it falling gracefully out of God's vast, open treasure chest in the sky, zig-zagging its way down, landing effortlessly into my waiting hands. Whenever I get paid in cash (which I love), I feel the bills with my hands, look upwards, and thank God. I know that they just landed fresh into my hands from God's treasure chest. God's fingerprints are all over them. I let money be the thing that keeps me connected to God. Money is the medium of my faith. It makes me cock my head back and beam my shining eyes right up to Him in gratitude.

Let's talk about money. I wish Salt-N-Pepa wrote that song. Because when we stay quiet about money, fear and shame fester inside. Let money loose, toss it around, be playful with it.

> *Our relationship with money sits right in our first chakra, our root chakra, near our genitals. It is that personal and that Sensitive.*

Otherwise, money can turn you into a crazy person. No matter how much or how little you have.

Money is many things. Money is metal, paper, and plastic. It clinks, it folds, it slides, it transfers. But money is mainly something else. Money is a feeling, an energy. We all hold our money inside an emotional wallet. Whatever emotional wallet you hold your money in is how it will show up in your life. The same way we have a life-long relationship with ourselves, our bodies, with God and with family. We have a life-long relationship with money. There is no getting away from it. Money is a secret relationship, a hushed conversation. Money whispers its breathy messages in our ears all day.

Too little money has desperate energy: "Will I be able to pay rent and buy groceries? Will I end up homeless and toothless on the street?"

Just enough money starts to sound panicky: "Will I always have enough money, or will I lose it and have to go back to the above, which was terrible?"

Too much money can turn paranoid: "Will people love me only for my money? Will my kids not be motivated in life because of all this money? How will I manage all my money? Will I be stalked and pursued for my money? Who is that freak walking behind me?" If you hold your money inside these desperate, panicky, or paranoid wallets, how can you become friends with it? You do not even trust it!

Money is a feeling, an energy

How can you learn to trust

money? There is a way. I learned it from the Jews in the desert. Whichever of the above categories you currently find yourself in, start doing what they did every day. *Look up to the sky.* The *Mun*, the manna, fell **every day** from the sky, not once a week or once a month, Every Day. Why Every Day? To remind us that every-single-dollar, every-single-day, comes from **One Place**. *And the same God who always provides is the same God who will always help us figure out how to manage what He gives.*

Money is the new *Mun.* They even sound the same. Both are the mechanism to build a constant rapport with God. Asking, receiving, and thanking, on the daily. Use whatever money situation you are in to develop a stockpile of faith in God; A Trust Fund. Hold your money lovingly inside a playful gratitude wallet and see what happens to the relationship. Watch how fat that wallet gets.

The best guidance I have heard about money and success came from Jim Carrey. He said something that changed me. He said:

"How will you serve the world? What do they need that your talent can provide? That's all you have to figure out. I can tell you, from experience, the effect you have on others is the most valuable currency there is."

What is he talking about, what is this *effect you have on others*? It can only be one thing — your Soul. The soul of other people can only be affected, can only feel something, if it is coming out of yours. **Your soul is what moves theirs.** Figure out how to use the things that naturally stir your soul to stir the soul of others. Engaging and perking up other souls around you, this is the valuable currency Jim is talking about. People will pay good money to feel their soul get stirred. I know I would.

Jim is the perfect example of this. He puts his entire essence into his soul's purpose: making us laugh. And he makes me laugh so hard. You can do this with any profession – a cop, a baseball player, a garbage man. We all know when we witness someone engaged and alive inside the work they do. We are drawn to it — mesmerized by it. I think of the viral videos of cops dancing as they direct traffic. When someone else is lit up and playful, it lights us up too. Their alive soul wakes up our dormant soul. And most of all, reminds us to be that way in our own lives. *I need your grace to remind me to find my own* (Snow Patrol).

Working in the service of touching souls — that is all we need to do. And the good news is that you can choose any activity to do it. The monetary success that follows comes only from God. But from what I have seen, the money flows where the authenticity is. Where the soul is. People will pay to be near that. It is a rare and enchanting gem. Authenticity feels like freedom. Authenticity has souls rise up. I love when music makes my soul feel something authentic. Ed Sheeran and Dermot Kennedy come to mind. Any person with musical ability can get propelled into super-stardom when they close their eyes and take the risk of singing from their Soul. Your ears always know it.

In dentistry, when I keep the interactions with patients clean, light, and free from manipulation, calculation, or the need to micromanage any specific outcome, I feel myself operating from my most authentic place. Authenticity derives from doing the right thing for every person, every single time, for its own sake. Presenting information playfully and calmly, then letting them decide. This lets me sit back and watch how the money takes care of itself. If I am driving in one lane, minding my own business, the money is in the next lane over, steering its own wheel. We can smile and wave at each other. The money drives its own car. I just keep my eyes on the road ahead, doing the next right thing. I ride shotgun to my soul's built-in navigation. Intuition comes standard in all vehicles.

When I put my real and weird self into what I do, I see how it becomes irresistible to people. And money cannot help but follow. People just want a real person, a human being, to be their dentist.

Figure out the things you enjoy **being** and **be** those things — as you do your job, whatever the job may be, it does not matter. For me, I love **being** calm, warm, spiritual, and playful. I am my most authentic while **being** these things. When I remember to **be** these things as I connect to my patients, I feel myself having a good mood day and the dentistry comes out better.

I also remind myself that I am a channel of God. I relax and let Him work through my hands. I think people can feel this relaxed energy, too. I have the specific privilege of being able to lay my hands on people and I honor that very much. Hands hold so much energy inside them. Touch transfers electricity. I always ask Him to let my touch be healing for whatever this person needs. I hold their head right near my heart.

If you ask God to work through you, He always will. He needs people. We are His manpower, his ground crew.

We are His hands and feet on the ground. God is always on the prowl for some good help. Sometimes, when I am done, I will look at the cosmetic bonding I just did on someone's front tooth and know *for sure* that it was not me. I am not *that* good. It was God. And it is a great feeling, getting used like that.

Chapter Twenty-One

Intention

Growing up as little Orthodox Jews, our teachers always reminded us to Daven with Kavanah (pray with intention). The energy of this innocent-sounding statement registered inside the soft gray matter of my developing brain as a threat: concentrate hard on every word you pray — or else!

When I Woke Up, I worked out the real meaning of Kavanah.

Kavanah = Setting your intention for the sake of Connection.

Kavanah applies to every single word we say and every single deed we do, not just in prayer. All we do, all day long, has ONE REAL GOAL: Connection with God and with other people.

Other people are different avenues and different routes that we take to arrive at one destination, God at the Center.

Intention is the *Prana*, the life force, you infuse into your speech and actions to elevate them from unconscious to conscious. The extra few seconds of weighted and measured breath that help you live your life on purpose. Breath is the amniotic fluid that slows us down, surrounds us, and puts us in a suspended state of bliss.

Intention comes down to one simple method: Take a breath, direct your heart towards heaven and hold imaginary hands with God in whatever you are thinking, saying, or doing.

Any action that derives Intention from your higher self, from Love, from God, carries unstoppable power in this world. Any action, delivered with Kavanah, to a plant, mineral, or animal will make it thrive. Pregame it. Take that three-second pause to open your **heart space** and focus a laser beam of love on your next target. Both of you will benefit.

Setting Intention helps to differentiate Soul from Ego. When we clarify our intention, we can observe that little friend within us called Ego. Ego can be a beast if we do not understand its purpose. Ego is here for balance. Ego is here so our soul does not get trampled on, so we have a voice. Ego wraps a protective skin around our formless soul. Ego gives us shape as distinct individuals with needs. It molds our lump of clay. Ego also drives accomplishment.

For the Ego to function properly, it must be tempered by the soul. Anita Moorjani teaches that both knobs, Ego and Awareness, should be turned up to level 10, so we can live in balance. The Soul and the Ego must constantly check in with each other.

For example, I ask my Ego, why am I writing this book? Am I writing this book for recognition or to spread love of Hashem? Am I feeding my Ego or my soul? Some days it is one, some days it is the other.

> *When we clarify our intention, we can observe that little friend within us called Ego*

They both get me to sit at the computer. When I take the time to set my Intention right, when it is my soul doing the writing, the book will carry the higher power I want it to have. The power to enter your heart.

On the Food Network show *Chopped*, chefs are competing against each other. They each get interviewed at the beginning of the show. A few common themes always pop up. You hear chefs say they want to prove to their parents or themselves that they picked the right career. Some want bragging rights. Some want their wives or kids to be proud. One key phrase always perks me up: one competitor will utter the magic words; *I just love cooking.* I put my money on that chef. No one can match the unmistakable flavor that *intention of soul* cooks into the food. Ego does not taste the same.

My soul's Intention in writing, when I am really connected to God, is to commit to paper the thoughts that illuminate and electrify my insides, in the hopes that reading these thoughts will do the same for yours. My Ego's Intention, on the other hand, is for you to think I am smart. I jump between the two all the time. The work of life is to constantly reset my Intention, always fine-tune those two knobs.

When it comes to being Jewish, Intention is a game changer. Judaism is an extreme sport. Lots of getting up early and disciplined practice. Entire playbooks and rulebooks to memorize. It can feel oppressive without understanding why we play this difficult sport. What is the one goal we are all sweating for? Connection to God. Period.

V'atem Hadevakim Ba'Hashem, Chaim Kulchem Hayom. All you people, the Clingers to God, Life for all of you, Today!! (Deut. 4:4) We all want to be players on the team of Life.

This is why I am in the game. To connect my open heart to God in real time, as I practice the sport of Judaism. The nonstop physical demands were a brilliant move by God. Why not just have us sit, meditate, and contemplate God's Glory all day? Because God knew better.

God knew that physical movement is our constant state and God capitalizes on that. He gave us things to smell, taste, feel, shake, wrap on our arms, eat, not eat, drink, not drink, wear, not wear, say, not say, candles to light, bread to bake, water to dunk our bodies in, and about 600 more things. The goal is NOT to do everything perfectly (which can cause serious religious OCD), but to have a million different ways to be constantly connecting. To **embody** the spiritual connection, to siphon God down into every cell of the body, to have us jumping from one connection to the next.

Buried inside every mitzvah is a red-tipped match that we can hold to the flame of God and feel it catch fire inside us. Every Mezuzah on every doorway we walk through presents to us another physical opportunity to reach for God. God constantly describes Himself Anthropomorphically in the Bible, with human features, like eyes, hands, and hearts. He has none of those things. So why is He describing Himself like this?

Because He understands our nature. He knows that our most relatable connection to Him will be this way, through imagining Him on our terms. If we think of Him as energy or as vapor in the mist, we will not be

We will lose the next generation of Jewish kids if we transmit all these heavy physical instructions without any emotional ones. Fear was once enough to keep the religion going, but that is not working anymore. We are losing too many.

I was once on the phone with a friend discussing how crazy it is that we ask our kids, at just 20 years old, to make the three most major decisions of their lives.

Where will they live?

Who will they marry?

What job will they choose?

These three pivotal decisions set the course for their entire lives! These are the watershed decisions. My friend said something to me I will never forget. She said, There is a fourth question you are leaving out. A fourth question that binds the other three together:

What goal do you intend to accomplish while answering those first three questions?

Whoa. I never thought of that. I never thought to use that level of mindfulness. To ask myself the deeper question. The *why* that lies under the surface of all the *whats, wheres and whens.*

I don't know the answer my 20-year-old self would have given to that fourth question, no one asked me back then, but my 40-year-old self-blurted out this reflexive answer: *Connection to Hashem.* This is the driving force behind everything I do. It is my singular and persistent answer to the question of *why I do anything*? To keep Hashem squarely fixed at the center of my life.

This is probably the most important question we can ask ourselves at any age and for any important decision. The question of Intention:

What is the *Why* that stands silently behind everything you do? What is *your* Why?

able to conjure the same Intimacy with Him. We need to picture Him a breathless lover we can kiss, or a best friend we can embrace. We need to imagine a physical God because that is our mental limitation. Seeing God as a person, with the same features and emotions we have, is our imagination's best device in this life to grab hold of Him. He knows this and allows this. So go there with Him.

Judaism is a very sensory experience. God engages every single sense, head to toe. This is how He gets the connection juices going, by asking us to fully engage our body. The involvement of heart and soul that follows is entirely up to us. That is the free will we have. Will our souls join forces with the physical practice of our bodies? This is the pathway of connection. Outward to inward. The physical sensations of our bodies transmit the feelings to our hearts, then our hearts pass along that energy to our souls. BODY—> HEART—>SOUL.

It goes something like this:

> *Close your eyes and smell the rose.*
> *Feel the pleasurable sensation tingling in your heart.*
> *Look up to the Creator and feel gratitude stirring in your soul.*

The key is to share the experience with God. Anything that falls short of this last part will leave you feeling incomplete, one stop short of a bliss-connection.

The missing piece I felt as a child and teenager was how to do this last part right, how to connect. I was taught all the physical rules, but they were handed to me wrapped inside intimidation and fear.

Do all these 613 things or you will be punished! I know one thing for sure, connection gets snuffed out inside fear.

I felt a weird void as a teenager, especially on Sunday afternoons. I did not know what to call it back then, but I remember feeling a vague sense of loss: hollow, empty, lonely. A low level depression. Now I know what to call it. *A Connection Void.*

I was emotionally disconnected from a Real God and from the adults in my life. No one was actively engaging me in emotional conversation or eye contact. Everyone seemed busy, distracted, and in their own little world. No one was modeling for me, in ways I could understand, how to connect to God or other people with love. So, my soul hung inside the void, detached and lonely.

When you take the time to connect with kids, you are throwing them a life-preserver. When kids learn how to connect to themselves — inside, and to others — outside, they will have an endless supply of resilience.

A serious epiphany:

The words Connection and God are the SAME THING! Connection is God and God is Connection. Teaching kids the art of Connection is teaching them God. This is our most important job as adults.

The best way to safeguard a child from a life that can fall into loneliness, suicide, or addiction, is to model skills of Connection. Talk playfully to God out loud in your kitchen and in your car. Let them witness how real He is to you. Talk playfully to them the same way. Look them in the eyes. Ask them how their day was and how it made them feel.

Chapter Twenty-Two

Perspective of Soul

Whenever you find yourself stuck inside a painful emotion, memory, or reality, realize this:

You are viewing the situation from the eyes of your body. Figure out how to flip that lens; learn how to see the same emotion, memory, or reality from the *perspective of your soul.* This spiritual backflip has the power to bring you something we are all after — true and lasting Comfort. A spiritual vantage point lands us in the holiest of destinations: a place of Meaning.

Our human senses are so limited. Our human capabilities can only perceive a thin slice of a vast reality. The least proof of this is that there is a whole world taking place behind the back of your head right now that you will never get to see. Jordan Peterson captures this concept gorgeously in his book *12 Rules for Life*: "We perceive a very narrow slice of a causally interconnected matrix, although we strive with all our might to avoid being confronted by knowledge of that narrowness."

Get outside the narrowness of your physical body. The one that only accepts the one version of reality right in front of its face. Drop the body and slip inside the vastness of your soul. We all have access to this inner ocean. There are many deeper sides to reality that we can perceive from the perspective of our soul. Close your physical eyes to open your spiritual ones.

Go inside to gain access to the Milky Way of your own Eternity. Behind your closed eyelids is an open space, a galaxy, for God's perspective to filter in.

If you are in pain, know that you are in human mode, and slowly shift gears to soul.

Human perspective says: Her life was cut short. She was taken too soon.

Soul perspective answers: This was how it was always supposed to be. We just did not know it. Her life was exactly as she planned it out with God.

Human perspective says: It is taking me so long to fulfill my dream of moving to Israel.

Soul Perspective answers: Everything is unfolding on time and exactly according to plan.

Which thought made you feel more relaxed and settled?

Create your own standby, at-the-ready thoughts that shift you back to the perspective of your soul. Overwrite old neural pathways that have always led you to pain. Formulate new soothing thoughts that know the quickest route to pull you out of pain. Only you know the words that will work best for you.

My patient lost her 17-year-old sister in a car accident. She was sitting in my chair a few weeks later, fresh from the tragedy. I summoned the courage to ask her, "What is the thought that you use to comfort yourself?" She answered right away, "This was the life she was always supposed to have. Not one minute more. Every soul has a purpose, and she must have accomplished hers quickly."

That was Perspective of Soul in motion.

We come in and out of this all day. It is impossible to stay inside *Perspective of Soul* 24/7. But the more often we reach for it, the more automatic it becomes.

I came across a few comforting thoughts to help heal the wounded soul. I hope they resonate with you, like they did with me. Try to *feel* the words as you read them. They go like this:

1. "Every age you have ever been is inside you."

    Mitch Albom said this to Oprah in an interview quoting Morrie. It is such a good one. When I get worried about getting older this thought reminds me that nothing is ever lost. I still have my vibrant, carefree 17-year-old and my sweet, innocent 4-year- old inside me. I will never lose them.

    There is an interesting phenomenon I have noticed about age: The people I grew up with never look old to me. I can always make out their young faces inside current pictures of them. But, the people I only met later in life, I cannot picture their faces young. I'm not sure what this means, but it makes me treasure the people I grew up with because I can still find their 10-year-old self in their 40-year-old face. It has always there.

2. God can remove any obstacle, easily.

    I once lived this hyper-vivid experience, so I can go back and revisit the emotion in my memory whenever I want to.

    It happened like this. My dream has always been to move to Israel and be a dentist there. In order to practice dentistry in Israel, there was a grueling dental exam I had to pass. It was the thing that loomed overhead and gave me the most anxiety about moving to Israel. Every dentist I know who took it failed, at least twice. Then one day, out of nowhere and due to no effort of mine, I got the news that the government decided to do away with the exam. If you have been practicing dentistry anywhere for more than five years, you get automatic reciprocity of your dental license. And just like that — Poof, the obstacle vanished. Thinking about this miracle still makes me shake my head in disbelief. Anything is possible with God. Everything is easy with God.

3. God keeps track of EVERYTHING, so I do not have to. Every detail of every story is written down. Nothing is lost to history. It is not my responsibility to remember every detail. Every life story, every picture, every video is held inside God's memory.

4. We live inside God's world. God lives inside ours.

5. All things are easy for God, so be still and let him do His thing.

6. I am God's favorite. You are God's favorite.

7. Everything is always working out easily for me.

8. God uses other people's mouths to speak to me. God uses my mouth to speak to other people.

9. God speaks to mo through thoughts and ideas that I think are mine.

> *God keeps track of EVERYTHING, so I do not have to*

10. When I give God my full attention, God gives me His, instantly.

11. The music in heaven has words. I hate music without words.

12. There is dancing in heaven. How could there be a world with no dancing? That would be hell.

13. There is laughter in heaven. I just know it.

SOME LIFE HACKS
To increase calm, breathe
To increase clarity breathe
To increase connection, breathe
To increase pleasure, breathe,
To increase pain relief, breathe
Negative thoughts are...optional
Judgmental thoughts are...optional
Critical thoughts are...optional
Scared thoughts are...optional

(I say the word 'optional' in my head the same sing-song way Elaine said it to Jerry in the *This and That* episode. "Spending the night is...*optional*")

Try to think only good and loving thoughts about any person in your life and watch them slowly rise to meet those thoughts. Seeing only their light and holding the best version of them inside your imagination helps that reality drop down to them from heaven. The wife of a man with no tongue once said to me, your spouse can wake up a different person each morning. Never give up hope. This is exactly how you can help. By holding the highest vision for their life.

Always remember — the twinkle in your eye and the flirt in your voice makes you irresistible to yourself and other people. This is what keeps you fresh, juicy, and delicious.

PEACE

There is one thing that can ensure peace in the world. Do you want to know what it is? Peace in the home. If every home in this generation had peace inside it, the generation after would know a time of peace in the whole world.

Peace in the home starts at the top. Parents set the tone for the entire house. Kids are never at fault. When they misbehave, they are only acting out the chaos they are feeling inside. They came to us as innocent souls. Our unconscious behavior created this chaos within them. This is not to place blame on us but to understand the urgency and importance of waking up and creating a cocoon of safety for them to rest in, especially after a hard day of being out there in the world.

What makes a home safe? Two things: good communication and good moods.

Kids need to be able to rely on these two things every day. These are the two pillars of peace. Take a course, read a book, get some therapy, work on yourselves in any way you know how. This will save the lives of your children.

> *Peace in the home starts at the top. Parents set the tone for the entire house. Kids are never at fault*

When children act out, run away, or take drugs you can be sure there is a problem with peace in the home. A glitch in communication or moods inside that house. During the height of discord in my marriage, when my husband was at his most controlling and angry, I found out later that one of my kids smoked pot in their room every night for a year. I do not blame that child. The fumes were better in their room than the fumes in the rest of the house.

Unconscious adults in the home create environments full of tension and strife inside the one place that should be a sacred reprieve for kids. I remember the way my husband and I fought, and it makes me want to cry for what it did to the little precious nervous systems of my developing children. I hope the love and peace we have achieved now can retroactively heal their souls from whatever damage we did.

God says he will only rest his Presence inside a home that has Peace. There is a palpable uncomfortable feeling hanging in the air, when a couple is fighting, that even God cannot tolerate. Even He has got to get the hell out of there. You literally do not know where to put yourself when you are near a couple stonewalling or being nasty to each other. This is another proof that we are made in God's image, because neither does He.

God calls peace between husband and wife 'Shalom Bayis,' Peace of the House. Why not Shalom Ish V'isha? Peace between Man and Wife? Because the parent's relationship is not contained in one room. The state of the relationship fills up the four walls of the entire house and affects everyone inside. The same is true of a peaceful house: the moment you walk in, you immediately savor the energy of that homey bliss.

Gila Jedwab

REACTION TIME

My youngest son went on Amazon and ordered himself a stop clock that measures time down to a tenth of a second. He was trying to achieve his personal best on the Rubik's Cube. (There is a Rubik's Cube championship happening somewhere in the world right now.) Ask any Olympic swimmer just how important one-hundredth of a second is.

For me, I work on shaving milliseconds off something else. Something I call my Reaction Time. This is the time it takes, measured in hours, minutes, or seconds, during crisis, difficulty, or even joy, to remember to re-engage with God. My only competition is myself. My training goal is to turn my mind towards God as quickly as possible, until it becomes an automatic reflex. Until I get my time down to a split second.

When I cannot find my keys in the morning

When I see a beautiful sunset at night

When I hear bad news

When I hear good news

When I cannot get my matrix band down (for the dentists)

When I lose patience at the way my husband is snoring

When I want to yell at the kids about the dog poop left on the front lawn

When my printer is jammed

When my computer freezes

When I am on hold with customer service

For some reason I resist turning to God in those moments to ask for His help. I let my stubborn self get stuck inside the agitation. I think, "I can find those keys on my own" Or I think, "I am justified in losing it over the dog poop." The second I pry myself out of the grip of the moment and turn to God for help, the tension eases its hold on me. Whatever I do next will be a lot calmer.

Jews say something that helps us improve our reaction time. Whenever we hear news of a death, we immediately say to each other, *Baruch Dayan Ha'Emet*. Blessed is the True Judge. Even though uttering this phrase sometimes feels impersonal or insensitive to me, I still do it. I think its purpose is to remind us to reflexively turn to God. It helps improve our overall collective reaction time.

In September of 2015, there was a group of Hasidic boys on their way to pray at Ma'arat Hamachpela. They took a deadly turn into a dangerous part of Hebron. The area with the red signs that say in Arabic: No Jew Gets Out Of Here Alive.

In a matter of minutes their tiny rental car was surrounded by an angry mob of Palestinians attacking them with stones and firebombs. Their car caught fire. The only choices the boys had were to jump out and be slaughtered by the mob or be burned alive in the car. I read an interview with one of the boys.

This boy caught my soul's attention. He said that as the chaos was happening all around him, he called out "Aibishter" from inside the burning car. Out of nowhere, a Palestinian man by the name of Fayez Abu Hamdia appeared on the scene and pulled them out through the car window. He escorted the boys through the angry mob and up a small hill to his house.

He gave them protection and water to drink until the army showed up to extract them. The part of the story that hit me was that this 19-year-old boy, inside his moment of acute terror, remembered to call out to God. This could only come from the culmination of having called out to God enough times in his normal, calm life that it became an embedded reflex in his limbic mind. That is Gold Medal Reaction Time.

Dr. Mary Neal did the same thing. When she was pinned underwater by her overturned Kayak in Chile, she remembers saying four simple words to God in those trapped moments: "Your will, not mine." What could have been moments of total panic for her became moments of total peace because her mind went straight to God. I often wonder about the daily practice of faith that this woman must have to get her this game-time ready.

I stub my toe and I forget to turn to God.

I find my lost keys or a really good parking spot and forget to thank God.

The acute anxiety we are feeling inside a panic attack comes from forgetting one thing — our unbreakable connection to God.

We are inseparable from Him. God promises at least twice in the Bible to never let us go, abandon us, or destroy us (Deuteronomy 4:31 and 31:6). However long it takes you to recover the feeling of this Eternal Connection, that is your baseline Reaction Time. You can start working on it today.

Rabbi Gavriel Sassoon was another tremendous teacher of Reaction Time for me. He lost 6 beautiful children in a tragic house fire in 2015. At their funeral, less than a day later, he was not questioning God at all. He was not angry, bitter, or blaming. He was only talking about one thing, Surrender. He was eulogizing in a low, keening tone, reminding us all that whatever happens is always God's will, not ours, and to accept it. It felt as if God Himself held a microphone under his lips to teach us about Surrender.

In an interview a few weeks later, he said the most

profound thing I have ever heard about Surrender. He said that there are some days that he needs to surrender every five minutes. It is never one and done. It did not take him years to reach that initial surrender, it took him half a day. But even a person already on this ultra-high level of Surrender admits to us that he still needs to practice it every day. I wonder about the connected life Rabbi Sassoon must have cultivated within himself to have the Superhuman Reaction Time he displayed at the funeral. I think about it all the time.

Rabbi Sassoon did another astonishing thing. He refused the tranquilizer medicine offered to him after receiving the crushing news. He said, "This pain is my Avodah (my work)." He instinctively and immediately knew that he needed to feel the pain and use it as a means to connect to God. This man understood that the faster you turn to God from inside the pain, the faster you will feel God's help, comfort, and healing come in. This is Sacred Alchemy. *The Art of transforming pain into connection. Fear into faith.* This is the work of life, the reason we came— to transmute base emotions into pure gold, by feeling their weight, and then lifting them to God.

Chapter Twenty-Three
God's Paradox

A paradox, according to Google, is "a seemingly absurd or self-contradictory statement that when investigated or explained may prove to be well-founded or true."

God is the mother and the father of all paradoxes: He is everywhere and nowhere.

Inside everything and above everything (Immanent and Transcendent).

He is my imaginary best friend and my REAL best friend.

One reality does not detract from the other. Both can peacefully exist side by side.

How do I know this? Because my own paradoxes peacefully coexist within me. And the truth of one does not detract from the truth of the other. This is another example of how our inner worlds are a reflection of God's. This comforts me. I used to think all parts of me had to make sense. Turns out, they do not.

Some of my Paradoxes:

I am super spiritual and super practical.

I am grateful and longing.

I am content and unsettled.

I am ditzy and smart.

I am stubborn and flexible.

I am mature and very immature.

Rabbi Aryeh Kaplan illuminated God's paradox in his book *Jewish Meditation*. I finally was able to wrap my mind around it.

He presents the two most common adjectives used to describe God-Blessed and Holy-*Baruch and Kadosh*.

Every blessing that leaves a Jew's mouth begins with the words, *Baruch Atah*. "Blessed are You."

What is this word, *Baruch*, that mindlessly rolls off my tongue a hundred times a day? I never really thought about it.

When people bless other people, they don't start with, "Blessed are you." We invoke this only with God.

"Blessed are you," according to Rabbi Kaplan, means "Immanent are you." Which really means, "You are found inside everything."

Baruch Atah is the entry point for whatever we are about to bless, from an apple to lightning. We begin by acknowledging that God is inside all of it. His Immanence permeates every molecule of creation.

I noticed something equally astounding. God allows us to address Him **super informally** with the pedestrian word "You." Why does the Master of the Universe diminish His own honor? I can think of only one reason. He is seeking our intimacy.

Holy is another word that I mumbled blindly my whole life. I never understood the tangible meaning of it. What does the word Holy actually mean?

Rabbi Kaplan cleared this up for me, too.

He explains Holy to mean Transcendent: existing above and separately from all things.

The word Transcendent allows me to go back and understand the word Holy. Transcendent is more concrete; my brain can hold it.

My light bulb goes off. Ah, Holy means He is up there. Blessed means He is down here. As it turns out, Blessed and Holy (Immanent and Transcendent) are opposites.

Now, whenever I say Blessed or Holy, my imagination can conjure a picture for the words I am saying.

Immanent, inside all things. Transcendent, above all things.

The real Aha Moment hit me when I realized that the most popular nickname of God, that rolls off our collective Jewish tongue, Ha'Kadosh Baruch Hu, (The Holy One, Blessed be He) is a cute and concise moniker of this exact paradox. He is eternally both at the exact same time.

The truth is human beings embody both aspects of God's Paradox more than we realize.

WE ARE ALSO IMMANENT:

Scientist Dr. Neil Degrasse Tyson is famous for his wild enthusiasm in explaining to anyone that will listen that we are all made of stardust.

He exclaims,

> "I know that the molecules in my body are traceable to phenomena in the Cosmos, that makes me want to grab people on the street and say, "HAVE YOU HEARD THIS?!" He continues, "These molecules are in us because the Universe is, in fact, in us. We are stardust in the highest, exalted way."

Molecular science shows that we share 99.9% of our individual genome sequence with other human beings. We share 98.5% with chimpanzees. And 60% with a banana.

What I am trying to say is that the individual cells of our body are found in all of life. They are scattered up in the galaxy and sprinkled down here on the earth. Traces of our cellular substance are scattered inside all of creation. Understanding that our bodies are Immanent with all of life helps us grasp the possibility that our souls are too. Look into someone's eyes and you can almost feel how those eyes belong to you.

Namaste: my soul is found inside yours and yours, inside mine. If our bodies are made of the same stuff, it follows that our souls are too.

We know God created us Immanent like Him. Telescopes and microscopes magnify the proof that we are found inside everything. But is it also possible for us to be Holy like Him? I say, Yes!

Moments of Transcendence can be achieved when our soul uses this body in the service of God and Creation.

In fact, God gave us the explicit instructions on how to be Holy. Let me explain.

There are three different categories of Brachot, blessings, Jewish people say.

1. Blessings of praise.
2. Blessings before enjoying something physical, like food.
3. Blessings before carrying out a Mitzvah.

Only the blessings that belong to this third category carry the words,

> "*Asher Kidi'shanu—>B'Mitzvotav*"

> "That He made us Holy—>Through His Mitzvot."

The first two categories of blessings, the pleasure and the praise, do not contain this three-word invitation to Transcendence. Holiness seems to have one portal — through this third category, the mitzvot. God invites us to experience His Transcendent World through the 613 access points He set out for us in the Torah.

God says, "*Kedoshim Ti'hyu, Ki Kadosh Ani* — Be Holy, Because I am Holy (Leviticus 19:2)." God is constantly drawing up our companionship to Him in the Transcendent Realm through all these different Mitzvot.

Transcendence through meditation of the mind can be frustrating and elusive. Quieting the mind is hard work. You could meditate for years and never achieve the transcendent state that 60 seconds of lighting Shabbat candles or shaking the lulav can do for you. One Mitzvah done with heart can transport your soul straight to the Transcendent Realm with God. We do not need to escape the body in order to Transcend, we need to USE it.

> *Quieting the mind is hard work*

There is one fascinating difference between these two states. Immanence arises from a state of being, Transcendence arises from a state of doing. We slide out of the birth canal into our Immanence; our Maker made us this way. No effort was needed on our part to share cellular similarity with all of sentient life. As the verse says, "B'ruchim Atem La'Hashem — Blessed are you to God (Psalms 115:15)." We are Born Blessed in the eyes of God. The wording itself is passive — *Blessed* is a non- resistant state of being.

The opposite is true with Transcendence. Transcendence must be earned. It requires focus and intention. The wording itself is active: "Kedoshim Ti'hyu! Be Holy!" *Transcendence* is a verbal directive. Our Immanence was God's gift to us at birth, our Transcendence is our gift back to Him.

In the Parsha of Kedoshim, where the heavy prohibitions and instructions are laid out for mankind by God, there is an interesting repetitive refrain. When God is delineating all His firmest requests, from *don't lay with animals* to *be kind to the stranger,* God caps off 16 different sentences with the words, "I am God."

Why?

It almost sounds like the parent who demands his child make the bed and then barks out the demeaning expletive — because I SAID SO. But there is something much deeper going on here. When God repeats Himself twice in the Bible, it is always for a reason. Sixteen times, He is begging us to pick up on something foundational.

Maybe it is this — God's Mitzvot sometimes make sense to us, but mostly they do not. God incessantly repeats the refrain, "I am God" here among the heavy rules of life to hammer something home: *We need to do these difficult things and not ask why.* God said so, that's why.

There is a human pull inside us that always begs for more information. It takes a superhuman discipline to quiet that insatiable curiosity. To trust that God is the keeper of all satisfying answers. To know that if He gave away these answers, it would vanquish all free will from the face of the earth. We postpone the deep gratification of knowing for a later date. We carry out God's requests blindly and willingly, trusting it all makes sense to Him. Why, because He is God.

So, what is the reward, why do this? Because this massive leap of faith shoots our mortal selves, for a flash, into the Transcendent realm. For a hot second, inside a mitzvah, we become Holy like Him. We close our eyes, fulfill this strange request, and trust that an explanation awaits us at some later date.

Trust confers a Transient state of Transcendence on us. For a fleeting moment, we are suspended on high. We trusted God! So we got to jump up to where He lives. We fall back down to earth until we reach for it again inside another Mitzvah. Every time I light Shabbat candles, I pole-vault into that sweet space with God.

I trust God to be that masculine boyfriend who has blindfolded me and is leading me, by the hand, down a curvy path of tall weeds towards the greatest vista of my life.

There is one more huge lesson we can learn from God's paradox of Transcendence and Immanence. The lesson is this: all romantic love relationships thrive on the tension of this very paradox. Closeness and distance. A love affair must vacillate between two poles, love and longing. In her book, *Mating in Captivity*, Esther Perel explained this concept in her beautiful poetic prose. She illuminates,

"Love enjoys knowing everything about you; desire needs mystery. Love likes to shrink the distance between me and you, while desire is energized by it... Love is about having; desire about wanting. An expression of longing, desire requires ongoing elusiveness."

God keeps it fiery and alive with us by having both Proximity and Chase in our love affair with Him. He is elusive as hell, but also right here, mingled inside our breath. He is the greatest mystery *and* also the most understood secret of our heart. That is one hell of a way to keep a relationship on its toes.

Broken Heart

If life brings you the exquisite pain of a broken heart, do not waste it.

Come to God with your shredded heart in your hand and He will let you touch His face. I once had my heart broken so badly; I thought I would never be happy again.

I am proud of myself for one thing I did during that dark time:

I did not waste my time of deep sadness and despair, I used it.

I saw it as a time of widened opportunity. I connected to God from deep inside the pain and came out the other side holding His hand. When God promises, "Imo Anochi Ba'tzara" — "I am with him in agony (Psalms 91:15)," He means it. God gets down in the trenches with us, sits next to us. He puts His hand on our back. We can rest our tired face right in His neck.

My happiness did eventually come back. It came back different. Smarter. It came back more resilient. My happiness came back thermally bonded to God. I used the heat of my pain to seal the edges. No separating tool fashioned by man has the strength to pull us apart.

Pain made me One with God. Pain made us inseparable in ways Joy could never have accomplished. We were in the depths together. Only He and I know the wicked battle that went on inside me. We came through hell together, battled nameless demons together, and have not left each other's side since.

The Point

There is an invisible package we hold in our hands as we jump from this world back to the next. Back to the place we came from. This package carries one thing – the relationship we grew with God inside this lifetime, inside this body.

The relationship checklist looks something like this:

Did I trust Him

Did I talk to Him

Did I thank Him

Was I playful with Him

Did I open my heart to Him

Did I try to be like Him

Did I choose Him

Did I serve His Creation

Did I reflect His essence back to Him

Did I grow my Holiness by following His Mitzvot

Did I refine my character

Did I cling to Him

Did I create intimacy with Him

Did I show Him my broken heart

Did I ask him to heal all the places inside me that need healing

The package we transport across dimensions, inside our immortal hands, holds the answer to all these questions.

When we land safely on the other side, God dusts off the top of the package and says, "Let's see what you brought Me."

I will tell him,

"This is what I struggled to grow in that place where You were hidden from me. The place I arrived into sloppy, stupid and confused. I couldn't even remember who I was, where I came from, or who You were. This package is what I was able to accomplish despite my profound and utter amnesia."

Then God will pull me tight to Him, look me tenderly in the eyes and say, "Thank you for trusting Me and giving Me the benefit of the doubt during all those ridiculously confusing times. Thank you for looking around for Me in the dark – I know that was hard. Let's unite again in the most blissful way. I will reward you with Crystal Clear Clarity that reflects how beautifully you served Me and trusted Me. I will give you comfort, solace, happiness, encouragement, and exhilaration in the same way you did for others on earth. You did good. I will heal you, hold you, love you and make you laugh. We will sing and dance to any song you want. Let's do all this together and call it Heaven."

That initial inkling – when our consciousness first dawns about how little we really know and how stupid we really are – this is the moment when we begin to wake up. There is no going back after that. Knowing we are stupid is the only way to get smart. Owning our total ignorance with humor is the ground zero of spiritual awakening. Floating in stupidity confers the greatest gift: the free will necessary to forge authentic, self-earned connection to The Creator.

In other words, we are born stupid in order to choose Him. There is no better time or place to take advantage of that stupidity than right here and now. To enjoy every second of this precious life. That is why we are here. To bond with God from within the stupidity. That is how you wake up. Are you ready?

Ode to God

I woke up this morning in love with You

My heart tingled through my left shoulder

I feel you inside everything
In the perfect temperature of my hazy morning bed
In the first sip of steaming morning coffee
The crisp inhale outside
Every sensory pleasure
The neck of every baby
The crunch of fresh crust
Eye contact without words
In kindness
In hope
In longing
Especially that
I miss you on this side
I knew You so well over there
We were One
We all were
We forgot
We came here to remember
For the chance to remember
That the other side is Home
But Home is missing one thing
Choice
We dropped down to accomplish one goal
To choose You in every moment
To trust You in every moment
To earn the relationship for ourselves
I long for Your face
To rest my weary head on your shoulder
Then I look over at my beautiful husband
And I realize that I can

Poem by Gila Jedwab

The Logic of Faith

Atheists
Scientists
Non-believers
Live a life of logic

Logic
It is safe
It has process
With proof to back it up
It is real
It is true
It is also WRONG
Logic
Is life's biggest deception
Because where is logic for the unanswered questions?
Why hunger strikes globally
Why the innocent are murdered daily
Why the corrupt are in power
Why my fears never cower
Why the good die young
Why there is breathe in My lungs
Why some are physically unable
Why individuals are given a label
Why the universe never ends
WHY?
This I cannot comprehend
That is when you realize all you have is
Trust in a higher power with a plan that you can't make "sense" of because the real
Money is in faith
the truth is not something that can be understood rather felt in a wave of relief

for belief
that God knows the answers
There are answers
in a leap of faith

Therefore
To the
atheists
scientists
and all you non-believers
if you want answers
the only logical choice is faith

By: Sara Raizel Jedwab (2014)

About the Author

Gila Jedwab is a wife, mother, writer, columnist, and dentist living in Long Island, NY. For ten years, anytime a lightning bolt thought struck her from either her outer or inner world, she would write it down on a scrap of paper. Those scraps coalesced into this book. Writing is her favorite way of communing with God. She hopes every day to witness God's Great Reveal and to live in a time where fear is replaced with Love.